I Remember
LAURIER

I Remember
LAURIER
~

Reflections by Retirees on Life at WLU

Harold Remus, *general editor*
Rose Blackmore and Boyd McDonald, *editors*

Editorial Committee:
Robert Alexander, Loren Calder, Joan Kilgour,
Frank Millerd, Baldev Raj

WILFRID LAURIER
UNIVERSITY PRESS

We acknowledge the financial support of the Government of Canada through the Canada Book Fund for our publishing activities. The Editors and the Press thank Wilfrid Laurier University through the Centennial Steering Committee for making this publication possible.

LAURIERi[•I•]

Library and Archives Canada Cataloguing in Publication

I remember Laurier : reflections by retirees on life at WLU / Harold Remus, general editor ; Rose Blackmore and Boyd McDonald, editors.

Includes bibliographical references and index.
Issued also in electronic format.
ISBN 978-1-55458-383-6

1. Wilfrid Laurier University—History. 2. Wilfrid Laurier University—Employees—Biography. 3. Wilfrid Laurier University—Faculty—Biography. 4. Retirees—Canada—Biography. I. Remus, Harold [date] II. Blackmore, Rose III. McDonald, Boyd, 1932–

| LE3.W48174 2011 | 378.713'45 | C2011-905120-6 |

Electronic monograph.
Issued also in print format.
ISBN 978-1-55458-411-6 (PDF), ISBN 978-1-55458-412-3 (EPUB)

1. Wilfrid Laurier University—History. 2. Wilfrid Laurier University—Employees—Biography. 3. Wilfrid Laurier University—Faculty—Biography. 4. Retirees—Canada—Biography. I. Remus, Harold [date] II. Blackmore, Rose III. McDonald, Boyd, 1932–

| LE3.W48174 2011a | 378.713'45 | C2011-905121-4 |

Cover photo by James Hertel. Cover design by Blakeley Words+Pictures. Interior design by Catharine Bonas-Taylor.

Photo Album images kindly provided by Wilfrid Laurier University Archives and Special Collections, Bruce Fournier, Raymond Heller, Walter Kemp, Joan Kilgour, and Herbert Whitney.

© 2011 Wilfrid Laurier University Press
Waterloo, Ontario, Canada
www.wlupress.wlu.ca

This book is printed on FSC recycled paper and is certified Ecologo. It is made from 100% post-consumer fibre, processed chlorine free, and manufactured using biogas energy.

Printed in Canada

RECYCLED
Paper made from
recycled material
FSC   FSC® C103567
www.fsc.org

Contents

~

Recalling Life and Livelihoods
at WLU

HIS IS THE STORY—ACTUALLY, MANY STORIES—OF THE LITTLE university that could. It is told by some of those who devoted themselves to making "Last Chance U," first, a superb small liberal arts college committed to its students and to teaching and, then, to the growth, diversification, research, partnerships, and publications that characterize Wilfrid Laurier University today. Along with retaining the "Laurier Experience," those efforts have made WLU the first choice for thousands of some of the best and brightest, whether in the province of Ontario or from across Canada or internationally.

Constraints of space and funding, not to mention time and energy, have meant that sundry areas, events, milestones, and personalities—which readers might have hoped to see recognized in the personal accounts recorded here—could not be included in any significant way. For example, the music therapy program. Opera Excerpts and the annual full opera mounted by the Faculty of Music. Graduate studies and research, which increased significantly over the decades. Any number of innovative initiatives pioneered by WLU faculty. The co-op program in Business and Economics, which spurred applications in those areas. Notable chancellors, in addition to Maureen Forrester. Readers may expect to find these and still other areas and personalities not included here in the official history of the university by Andrew Thomson.

Readers may notice discrepancies between what one writer records or supposes and what another has set down. Where "facts" were at odds, we have tried to eliminate or harmonize discrepancies, but where there was no written record to resolve the issue, we were left with what were simply differing memories. Short of hauling the writers before the Retirees Assizes, for which we had no taste, time, or talent, we have let the discrepancies stand. As many memoirists have observed, when memory speaks it speaks to one audience in one voice and in another voice to a second audience at a different time and place—and that historical "truth" is sometimes best conveyed by a certain kind of "fiction" written from the heart.

Not surprisingly, the contributions in a volume such as this are diverse in content, viewpoint, and tone. Yet readers will note some common themes. Nostalgia for a small university where faculty, staff, and students were close and new initiatives were readily approved and easily implemented. Sometimes, bemused reflections on what happened or was allowed to happen—though sometimes definitely not. As *cantus firmus* a dedication to common goals, along with the hard work required to attain them and sometimes the work-arounds necessitated by tight funding. Pride in what developed from such modest beginnings and for having been a part of it all.

A glance at the table of contents makes clear that the gender balance is skewed in favour of male retirees. Given that the faculty in the early days was overwhelmingly male, as is attested in various of the contributions, it is not surprising that those we asked to write about those times are predominantly male. Unfortunately, some of the few women from those early days whom we would have wanted to write are no longer with us, for example, Grace Anderson, Helene Forler, Michal Manson, and Flora Roy. Given the essential role played by staff, we regret that some of those we invited to write were unable to do so. As this book was in process the Rev. Dr. Delton Glebe died at the age of ninety-two, the chapter he contributed to the book becoming part of his legacy to WLU.

Balance between areas and departments was another factor in issuing invitations to contribute. Some found themselves unable to do so because of other commitments or responsibilities or because of ill health. We are grateful—and were indeed surprised—that so many did in fact respond to our invitation to contribute a chapter to the volume. We thank all of them most sincerely. The General Editor especially expresses his gratitude to the contributors for their patience in responding to queries and suggestions about his edited versions of their chapters during the various back-and-forths to which he subjected them and to the other editors and the editorial committee for their creativity and resourcefulness in the conception and planning of the book and for their counsel, encouragement, and legwork along the way. He must assume responsibility for any errors in the editing of the chapters.

We thank James Hertel who, during his many years as university photographer, created the trove of photos from which, with the help of his unsurpassed technical skills and unfailing memory, the editors selected virtually all of the images that appear in the photo album at the end of the book and, in greater number, on the website of the Wilfrid Laurier University Retirees Association (www.wlu.ca/retirees). We are grateful to Cindy Preece at the Laurier archives for research along the way. To the archives we express our gratitude for permission to reproduce the photos. Ray Heller, Herbert Whitney, and Joan Kilgour each supplied a photo, and to them we are indebted also. Our thanks as well to Arthur Stephen for various of the photographs that appear on the retirees' website.

We wish to thank also the Centennial Committee of the university for the grant that made publication possible and Wilfrid Laurier University Press for their guidance and meticulous attention to detail along the way and for the superb craftsmanship represented in the volume that is a hallmark of their publications.

The contributions to WLU over many decades as represented by this small sampling of retirees (who in a few cases are alumni as well) are not only a "looking back." They constitute part of what Wilfrid Laurier is today as well as of the "looking ahead" that marks the university in its dedication to the search for truth in the conviction that *veritas omnia vincit.*

General Editor: Harold Remus
Editors: Rose Blackmore, Boyd McDonald
Editorial Committee: Robert Alexander, Loren Calder, Joan Kilgour, Frank Millerd, Baldev Raj

Part One

Foundations

Chapter 1

Money: Counting It and Making It Count

TAMARA GIESBRECHT

On March 9, 2011, Robert Alexander interviewed Tamara Giesbrecht, with assistance from her husband Roy Warren. Tamara Giesbrecht came to WLU at the point in its history when Waterloo University College ended thirty-five years of affiliation with the University of Western Ontario and became Waterloo Lutheran University.

Ms. Giesbrecht received an Honourary Doctor of Laws degree from Wilfrid Laurier in November 1981. In 1984 she was named to the Order of Canada. The investiture took place on October 3, 1984; the citation by the Governor General of Canada read in part, "The daughter of Mennonite refugees from Russia, she went to work at sixteen and advanced, through sheer management ability, to become Vice-President and Comptroller of Wilfrid Laurier University in Waterloo, Ontario. Her contributions to that institution's financial stability in critical periods have brought wide recognition of her astuteness and wisdom."

Q. Would you tell me a little bit about your background, where you were born and where you went to school?

A. My uncle was the mayor of Moscow, Russia. My father owned a meat-packing plant and was a salesman for Singer Sewing Machine Co. I was born in 1922 and had two sisters, one older, one younger. The political atmosphere became dangerous for us after the Reds overcame the White

Russians. Since our family was well-to-do, my father was scheduled for execution. But my father had treated his employees well enough that they helped him plead his case to the authorities. They were successful, so our family was able to leave. We used the Mennonite underground to get to Switzerland and then to Belgium. From there our emigration to Canada was sponsored by what was known then as the East End [now First] Mennonite Church of Kitchener. The George Eby family took us in when we arrived.

Father got a job with Singer, enabling us to buy a house between Cambridge and Kitchener. Sadly, he died within a year and a half of lung cancer, leaving us impoverished. Mother went to work while I took care of my sisters and a two-month-old brother; I was only three and a half at the time. When it was time for me to go to school, Mother took the night shift so she could be home to take care of the children while I was at school. I graduated from Kitchener Collegiate with some extra commercial courses.

Q. What was your first job out of the house?

A. I got a job at Cluetts shirt factory at sixteen. When the union came in, they wanted a closed shop and being Mennonite I wouldn't join. So they bypassed the piecework I was doing. Without anything to do, I had to resign. There was a new Eaton's store that was hiring, so I went for an interview. When he asked me why I left Cluetts, I said, "I refused to join the union." "You're hired," he said. I was in charge of the chinaware department; my job was to sell and order replacement stock, as well as to develop a clientele. I also sold appliances on the side.

I saw an ad for an accountant at the YMCA and was hired. (I didn't have all of the required credentials, but if someone asked me what my favourite thing to do was, I'd say, "I love counting.") Once, when the manager was unable to attend a board meeting, he told me to go the next day. I put on a black dress suit and a nice hat and showed up. All the male members were offended by my presence because I was only a high school girl with no special qualifications to be there. But they grudgingly gave me respect. Because of how I handled things, I was asked to be a permanent member of the board.

Q. How did you come to WLU?

A. Mother was unsettled and thought a change by going to Vancouver would help. So I said we should buy a car and I'd learn to drive. The driving instructor passed me but he was convinced I'd never make it. I got us all the way without ever making a left-hand turn. When Mother became unhappy there, we returned in the summer of 1960. I needed a job and Waterloo Lutheran University needed someone to do their books. President Villaume was already there when I was hired.

Q. What struck you about the job or the people when you arrived?

A. I started out by being given a box of bills—some paid, some overdue, some warnings of services to be cut off. I worked hard to straighten things out. I submitted my first budget and ended that year with a surplus. [In the words of President Neale Tayler at her retirement, this was the beginning of her reign as a "financial wizard."] The people I met and worked with were very helpful and I made good friends with many of them.

Q. What jobs did you hold while you were here?

A. I became business manager the next year and comptroller in 1963. Eventually I realized I didn't want to work with anyone who didn't have authority. The Board of Governors was strongly resistant, but after a day of to-ing and fro-ing with Chairman Harry Greb, they finally relented. In 1967 they made my position a vice-presidential post, which I then held until my retirement in 1978. I was the first woman on a university board in Canada.

Q. What was your financial method before you had access to provincial funds?

A. Having straightened out the mess when I arrived, I never wanted to let that happen again. I balanced the books every night before I came home, so I knew precisely what our situation was every day. That way I could handle any request as it came to me. Usually I came home at 5 p.m., but sometimes it took until 4 a.m. to finally clear everything up. The other thing I did was always pay cash and on time. I never borrowed, as most businesses did from time to time.

Q. But how did you manage to build so much, like the seminary and most of the library? Didn't you use mortgages for large capital projects as everyone else did?

A. No.

Q. How was that possible?

A. Well, the faculty and staff were wonderful about accepting significantly less in salaries than those down the street at Waterloo. I don't remember how much they gave up.

Q. I imagine they complained in the faculty lounge.

A. Yes, but they never made a public protest about it.

Q. What was it like to work with President Villaume?

A. It was interesting. I seem to remember he expected lunches to be made by his assistant, Arlette Peterson, at the oddest times. And sometimes it was tense because he often had conflicts with the faculty.

Q. What was Dean Lloyd Schaus like to work with?

A. He was a kind, thoughtful scholar, and very easy to work with.

Q. How and why did Waterloo Lutheran decide to go provincial?

A. Windsor had tried, I think, but it didn't seem to work. I didn't think we had much of a chance but we continued to think about it. The first problem was how we could convince the Lutheran synod to sell us the university while keeping the seminary for themselves. One night I had a revelation; I was going to borrow the money from the bank and offer it to the Lutherans. I told President Frank Peters about it the next morning. He didn't say much. Two days later he came into my office and said, "The Ontario Minister of Education has agreed to meet with us this Saturday."

Q. What did you think about that?

A. It was the first time I had borrowed money, so I wasn't sure that the bank would go along, but they did. I paid it back in less than six months.

Q. By the way, how was your relationship with Frank Peters?

A. He was very easy to work with. He was the opposite of President Villaume. He got along very well with the faculty. He had only taught here a very short time before he was chosen to be president.

Q. Getting back to the big change, how did you get the Minister of Education and the synod president to agree?

A. The government was very reluctant, because if they allowed us to switch, they felt they would have to allow other church universities, like Windsor and Ottawa, to switch as well.

Q. What convinced the Minister?

A. I think we ran our books so well that he couldn't convince others that we would be a bad risk. And we didn't ask for any extra catch-up money.

Q. What happened next?

A. We had to make an evaluation of what the university's share of the property was worth. We came up with about $3 million. And then I went to each congregation in the synod to present our case. I didn't think they'd accept it, but the vote finally came in our favour.

Q. And then the government accepted too?

A. Yes.

Q. And then other denominational universities followed suit?

A. Yes.

Q. How did this change your job?

A. It made things easier. We were able to raise the salaries of the faculty and staff quite soon afterward. And we kept moving forward with building plans.

Q. What else was different?

A. Well, I had to go to each property owner in our huge block and try to get them to sell. There was a farm, an ice business, and a cider mill. One of them was quite resistant, but he finally agreed, so we soon owned everything from University Avenue to King Street to Bricker Avenue to Albert Street, except for the southwest seminary property.

Q. What were some of the joys while working here?

A. I can't really think of any, though I certainly felt relief when we accomplished a major effort. And of course I loved working with many of the people. I especially remember Flora Roy's energy and ability to keep adding new things to our school.

Q. What were some of the trying times?

A. The members of a small town council from north of Waterloo were coming to me at WLU for financial advice. My assistants and I were a bit tense as we prepared for this meeting. They, however, had overindulged at their meal before arriving and were in no shape to ask for advice, much less to understand it. It was a total waste of time.

Q. Any more?

A. Yes. I remember one time when the architect came to see me. He was white as a sheet. He had found a gurgling spring under one of the buildings he was starting to build. I told him to fix the problem any way he could. It was the only time we told the board after we had spent a big chunk of their money, instead of getting their permission first.

Q. Can you share some memories of situations that you'll never forget?

A. When we decided to build the new gym, we just about gave them a blank cheque. I still remember how everything they got was the best available. That is how we ended up with an Olympic-size swimming pool. And that reminds me of ladders.

Q. Ladders?

A. Yes. Some students had come to me with a proposal to link two of the teaching buildings together with ladders. This didn't sound quite right, so I asked Reg Haney, our lawyer, to look into it. Our insurance company wouldn't cover the ladders, so I was able to refuse the students without appearing to be uncooperative.

Q. Anything else?

A. Yes. One day I told Millie Reiner, the dining hall manger, to go to Toronto and buy us a nice set of dinnerware for banquets. She came back with a beautiful set. I couldn't believe the bill; she paid about four times as much as I thought a really good set would cost. She and I laughed about that over the years. We hid the cost because we didn't dare tell anyone.

Q. What other responsibilities did you have over the course of your career?

A. In 1975 I was appointed by the Ontario government to the Ontario Council on University Affairs and served for two years as financial advisor.

Q. Finally, when and why did you leave WLU?

A. I retired in 1978, shortly after President Peters did, though it was not connected to his leaving in any way.

Q. Why?

A. I was tired. The job had been my life. I can't remember ever taking a vacation.

Q. How did you finish up your eighteenth year?

A. I left them a budget surplus, as I always did, this time of $6.2 million.

Q. That is amazing: eighteen surplus budgets. How have you spent your retirement, considering it began early in your fifties?

A. I had joined the Board of Directors of Equitable Life Insurance Co. of Waterloo in 1970 and continued with them until 2002. I also was available for financial consultations with WLU if they requested it. This ended with my helping them with a major pension issue, also in 2002.

Q. I have greatly enjoyed this time with you and Roy. Thank you for sharing your memories with the community. I know it will be appreciated by those who lived through these events, as well as those who are curious in years to come.

A. I enjoyed it myself.

Chapter 2

Waterloo College Student to University Lawyer: On the Legal Side of Things

REGINALD A. HANEY

I ARRIVED IN WATERLOO IN SEPTEMBER 1948 READY TO EMBARK on a new adventure: post-secondary education at a small institution called Waterloo College. The college was the Faculty of Arts and Science of the Evangelical Lutheran Seminary of Canada, which had been established by the Lutheran church in 1911. The seminary did not possess degree-granting powers, and in order to provide students with a wider range of course offerings and a degree upon graduation, an affiliation agreement had been entered into with the University of Western Ontario in 1925.

The late 1940s were exciting years. World War II was finally over, veterans were returning to the classroom, jobs were plentiful, and the mix of recent high school graduates with mature students, many of whom had seen action during the war, added an interesting dimension to classroom discussions, especially in history and political science. I felt at the time we had excellent professors. Flora Roy, Alex Potter, James Clark, Dorland Evans, and Bill Scott were five of my favourites, but there were many other caring and dedicated faculty.

In 1948 Waterloo College had approximately 225 full-time students, and by my second year I knew most of them. A strong sense of community developed within such a small student body. For most of us, our interests were not just academic, but social, athletic, and spiritual as well. Chapel was held in the mornings, there were many social events organized by the student council in the evenings and on weekends, and our football, basketball, and hockey teams were able to compete with the larger colleges and universities and enjoyed strong student support. No one who attended Waterloo College during this period would have left without having formed deep relationships with their fellow students, which in my case have continued from the time of my graduation in 1951 down to present day.

I did not enter Waterloo College with any preconceived notions about what I wanted to do following graduation. However, I did have a passion for education, which had been instilled in me by my mother, who had not been to university but was well aware of the importance of pursuing a post-secondary degree. As it turned out, Waterloo College proved to be a perfect fit for my personality and lifestyle. The college was small, class size was rarely more than thirty students, professors were approachable and available for consultation or just to talk; several even lived in residence with the students. The main building, Willison Hall, contained the classrooms, chapel, and library as well as common rooms where students could meet and discuss courses and sports or play cards if so inclined. The upper floor and most of the second floor constituted the men's residence; a house across Albert Street served as the residence for women.

Students who lived in residence were members of the boarding club and took their meals on the ground floor of Willison Hall. We were all assigned various duties such as setting tables, serving food, and washing dishes. Twice each year students assisted when trucks driven by volunteers collected food from various Lutheran churches over a wide area; included were preserves, potatoes, apples, and other such staples. These were stored in the basement of Willison and reduced our food costs considerably.

During my time at Waterloo College there were many amusing incidents. One in particular created quite a stir and ensnared two popular professors: Herman Overgaard and Flora Roy. In one of Professor Overgaard's early classes he passed around a paper on which all class members were asked to write their names so he could take attendance in each class. Someone entered the name of Dick Tracy and for the rest of the term whenever Herman took roll call, someone in the back row answered "here" for Dick. When Dick did not hand in his final exam and Herman asked him to stay after class the jig was up. Unfortunately, other professors started to check their class lists, and Flora Roy announced in her

English class that she too had a fictitious student, by the name of Morris Mortimer. When she announced this great discovery, it turned out Morris was a real person—who just happened to be my roommate. Great fun all round.

It was at Waterloo College that I first considered law as a career. This interest arose in the fall of 1949 during Frosh Week, when I was asked to act as defence counsel representing a number of first-year students facing various trumped-up charges who were required to appear before a kangaroo court. I received several acquittals and my roommate and others suggested that I should consider going to law school following graduation. The seed had been planted, and in September of 1951 I was enrolled as a first-year student at Osgoode Hall Law School in Toronto, and after completing the four-year course of study was called to the Ontario Bar in 1955.

After my call I returned to Waterloo and joined an established law firm, was made a partner in 1958, and was very pleased to see my name on the door. At about this time things were happening on Albert Street. In 1959 the Evangelical Lutheran Seminary of Canada, by an act of the Ontario legislature, became Waterloo Lutheran University with degree-granting powers, and Waterloo College passed into history. It was during this period that I established a solicitor–client relationship with WLU that continued from approximately 1960 for the next fifty years. In 1973 Waterloo Lutheran University underwent another major corporate change when by the Wilfrid Laurier University Act (1973), Wilfrid Laurier University assumed all university functions from Waterloo Lutheran University. With no change in acronym, WLU came to stand for Wilfrid Laurier University.

The legal issues that arise within a university community are similar to those that occur in any other community. These include contractual disputes, intellectual property concerns, criminal and quasi-criminal offences, property transactions (deeds, mortgages, and leases), legal opinions, and lawsuits, both for and against the university. One unfortunate lawsuit occurred in the 1960s when the Student Union sued the university, claiming ownership of the Student Union Building. This case went to trial and the court found in favour of the university. I did not rejoice in the result as I felt from the outset of the action that it would damage relations between the Student Union and the Board of Governors. There are other legal issues involving certain policies and practices which, as a rule, are unique to universities. These include academic freedom, tenure, and faculty and student appeals. These issues often resulted in contentious disputes sometimes ending in adversarial proceedings.

Prior to the 1970s very few disputes involving universities in Canada ended in court proceedings. If there were disagreements involving faculty or students, settlements were usually arrived at by mutual agreement, without resort to litigation. This situation changed with the passage in Ontario of a statute called the Statutory Powers Procedures Act (1971). The statute required tribunals empowered by an act of the legislature to make decisions affecting the rights of others to adhere to the basic rules of natural justice in arriving at their decisions. WLU had been incorporated by a provincial act and accordingly anyone empowered by the WLU Act to make decisions affecting others was bound to follow the rules set out in that legislation. These basic rules of natural justice required that the individual whose rights were in issue—for faculty, tenure and promotion hearings, for example, and for students' grade appeals and the right to remain in a program of studies—now had to be given reasonable notice of the hearing, the right to be heard, to be represented by counsel if they so chose, and the right to receive a copy of the decision. A new era had arrived, and the old way of dealing with on-campus disputes was over. After 1971, universities were required to re-draft most of their policies and procedures that affected the rights of faculty and students. As I reflect back on my many years as a university solicitor, it is this area—the application of the rules of natural justice—that I found the most interesting and the most challenging of the many cases I was asked to handle for the university.

All graduates of Waterloo College, Waterloo Lutheran Seminary, Waterloo Lutheran University, and Wilfrid Laurier University can look back on the first 100 years with pride in our universities' achievements and with gratitude for those individuals whose hard work, foresight, and dedication made this success possible. I believe a special tribute is owing to the early church leaders who established the seminary, created Waterloo College as the Faculty of Arts and Science in an agreement with the University of Western Ontario, and later established Waterloo Lutheran University, out of which grew two excellent universities, the University of Waterloo and Wilfrid Laurier University. During my many years at

WLU, first as a student, then as a professor and general counsel, the university has been blessed with strong leadership at the top, competent faculty and staff, and strong support and involvement from its students and alumni. I have every expectation that the next 100 years will be just as impressive for WLU as the first 100.

Chapter 3

The Bookstore Grows Up

PAUL FISCHER

O N THE WILLISON HALL DAYS OF THE LATE 1950S THE BOOKSTORE was almost literally a "closet" operation, open for only the few weeks of the year when books for courses had to be purchased. Then it moved to the original student union building, where it was managed by Elsie Fisher, who divided her time between the bookstore and the student newspaper. She was followed by Roger Seegmiller, who served until I arrived in late August of 1965. Elsie meanwhile had moved down University Avenue to manage the bookstore at the University of Waterloo. We had a great time trying to get publishers and other university bookstores to figure out which Fisher/Fischer was at which bookstore—which were said to be "a stone's throw apart." Years later, when Waterloo Lutheran University became Wilfrid Laurier University, another of the jokes circulating around the change in name was that "Laurier" was chosen so that the bookstore would not have to change the initials on its shopping bags.

I had served nine years in parish ministry when I was asked to take on the job of managing the bookstore. As an alumnus of both Waterloo College (1953) and Waterloo Lutheran Seminary (1956), I considered myself honoured to have been given this opportunity. It was a challenging career change and remained so for the twenty-eight years I had the job.

I arrived in the midst of the fall rush. I was very fortunate to have the capable assistance of Margaret Gellatly to coach me through it. By this time, the bookstore was located in the Torque Room, which was the coffee shop and gathering place in the basement of the Arts Building.

Textbooks were dispensed from a counter in the hall; paperbacks, stationery supplies, and other merchandise were sold on a self-service basis.

In the sixties, there had been a student sit-in at the bookstore at the University of Waterloo which resulted in the decision to discount textbooks. It was a big concern for us because the margin on textbooks is so small. We decided that we simply couldn't afford to offer a discount because we were mandated to recover all costs out of revenues. Because of this, we were one of the first university bookstores in Canada to get into the business of buying and selling used books and to expand our supply of used books through the Follett book company in Chicago.

With the support of the university and in the interest of further development, we became a member of the National Association of College Stores and I was able to take advantage of summer courses at their headquarters in Oberlin, Ohio, as well as attend seminars and conventions at places such as Las Vegas, Miami, and Chicago. Our membership in the Canadian Booksellers Association with its national conventions, trade shows, and seminars, and its strong contingent of university bookstores was also an important resource for us. One fall, we were able to use a lucky windfall from the sale of lottery tickets to send our entire staff to a university bookstore seminar. It was also my good fortune to have served on the board of directors and as treasurer of the association

Summer school and fall and winter extension courses were a significant part of WLU, both on campus and at external centres at Orillia, Barrie, Brampton, and Orangeville. This necessitated sending bookstore staff with cartons of books and cash registers to these locations for the sale of textbooks on weekends. For convocations we were the ones who took care of the rental of gowns to graduates, who increased steadily over the years.

The urgent need for expanded facilities was recognized by the university in 1970 when they provided an up-to-date, centrally located, attractive facility in the concourse between the Central Teaching Building, the new Student Union Building, and the cafeteria. All aspects of the bookstore services were brought together under one roof. No longer was it necessary to have campus shop items sold during limited hours from a dinky room in the former student union and textbooks from temporary locations during rush periods. It was the coming of age of the bookstore and a recognition by the university of the importance of a well-run, attractive bookstore as essential to the academic and cultural life of the university community.

None of this would have been possible without the expertise and dedication of the staff, which grew from three and a half to around twelve full- and part-time employees. At inventory time, rush periods, and convocations, we had a large number of part-time personnel, including students, whom we could call upon. It was absolutely essential for staff to work closely with faculty on required books and course packets, with the registrar's office for information on course enrolments, with the business office for accounting services, and increasingly with Computing Services. Sales increased from a quarter of a million dollars in 1965 to surpass the million-dollar mark during 1980 to over $3 million when I retired in 1993.

In October 1980 the bookstore launched an annual Meet the Author Series designed to introduce Laurier faculty and students as well as the community generally to some of Canada's illustrious authors who, in turn, had the opportunity to speak about their work, read from their most recent book, and autograph copies of their books, with the bookstore offering refreshments. The first author, Norman Levine, was not very well known, but his book *Canada Made Me* was hailed by Mordecai Richler as probably one of the best books about Canada. When John Fraser came to discuss his new book, *The Chinese: Portrait of a People*, the refreshments were egg rolls and tea. Eddie Greenspan arrived in a stretch limousine to discuss his book on the Demeter case. I recall him lighting up for the event even though there were signs prohibiting smoking. David Suzuki drew a huge crowd down at the Athletic Complex.

Peter C. Newman, with black tam and scarf, talked about the new establishment, and Margaret Atwood filled the pub at the top of the Student Union Building as did Alice Munro. When Pierre Berton was here, he surprised me by telling me that instead of turning his estate over to his many children, he was planning to give it to the writers' union. Jim Unger of the *Herman* books entertained students by creating cartoons on the spot to hand out to students who lined up across the concourse to get their books autographed. Maude Barlow inspired us to deeper loyalty to our country when we organized a celebration of Canada's 125th and gave out Canadian flags. Charlie Farquarson got us laughing and Al Purdy read his poetry to us as only he could. We also featured local authors like Edna Staebler and WLU faculty such as Terry Copp, Grant Head, and Barry Gough. Over the years it was like a who's who of Can-Lit. The generous support of the publishers for these events was very much appreciated.

In 1990 the campus shop merchandise was moved to rented space at the corner of University Avenue and King Street. It was an attractive retail outlet, called the Purple and Gold or sometimes the Hawk Shop, and it freed up more space in the campus bookstore. However, a few years later, in 1997, when some alterations were made at the bookstore it was moved back again and consolidated with the rest of the store.

It was a very interesting time to be on campus, with tremendous growth in numbers of students, faculty, and staff, expansion of the campus and construction of new buildings, and the growing pains accompanying the many and various changes. When I retired in January 1993, new technologies for assembling course material from several sources into custom-made manuals was coming, and there was a much greater emphasis on computers. I was happy therefore to make room for a younger generation. It was gratifying to me that Shelley Worden, who had been hired during my tenure, became manager for several years until she left to become the person responsible for the Follett used-book business serving university bookstores for all of Canada.

Today the bookstore is more than "just books," with sales of music and merchandise and computer equipment and software. But, as when I started, books—required and otherwise—are still at the core of its operations and continue to justify the name "bookstore." I am pleased and proud to have been a part of it for so many years.

Chapter 4

Odyssey: Waterloo College, Waterloo Lutheran Seminary, WLU

DELTON J. GLEBE

*W*ATERLOO COLLEGE AND WATERLOO LUTHERAN SEMINARY became part of my life as early as 1931, when I·was twelve years of age. My uncle Otto came from Hanover in his Dodge sedan to our fifty-acre farm near Neustadt to give us a ride to Waterloo. This was a rare and special event in the Dirty Thirties. Upon arriving in Waterloo we were travelling westward on Dearborn Street (now University Avenue) toward King Street. Uncle Otto pointed ahead toward a huge red brick building, looming up three stories tall like a castle. "That's Waterloo College and Seminary," he said. "That's where you should go some day."

Thirteen years later, in 1944, came my next significant contact with that building and that campus. After thirteen years of high school and a promising career in accounting and administration with an international packing company newly located in Hanover, I was on my way in my 1938 Pontiac to enrol in Waterloo College to prepare for entrance to the seminary. That Pontiac took me through six years of college and seminary and into the first few years of parish duties. It took Waterloo College co-eds to basketball tournaments at Western and a delegation of students and the dean of Waterloo College to a Lutheran student convention in Ann Arbor, Michigan. It also transported some of Dr. Ulrich Leupold's male chorus throughout eastern Ontario. Plus countless trips to Neustadt, the residence of my fiancée and my parents.

That red brick building—later called Willison Hall—was completely (and attractively) covered with green vines expressing warmth and welcome. It was home to both the college and the seminary. It housed everything! Classrooms, offices, male dormitory, library, chapel, gymnasium, dining room, storage, furnace room—anything and everything required for operating an educational institution.

My graduating class of twenty-five was the largest up to that time. I had the honour of being valedictorian. It was the University of Western Ontario that granted our degrees, but most of our exams were set and marked by the Waterloo faculty. In much earlier years, however, both Waterloo faculty and students had to write the exams set and marked by Western!

From those three years at the college (1944–47) various memories come to the fore. Recapturing effective study habits. Much time given to classical Greek. Occupying the coldest dormitory room. Participation in the Lutheran Student Movement on campus. Participation in the boarding club. The club was unique to the college. It was operated exclusively by us dormitory students. We hired the chef, procured all supplies, financed the operation, and annually collected a truckload of meats and vegetables from farmers in Bruce and Grey counties. The collectors enjoyed that glass of cider provided by some of the farmers. The boarding club, the dormitory, the relatively small enrolment, and all facilities embraced by one building helped to create a sense of community that lasted a lifetime. The graduates of the college became notably successful in the business and professional world as entrepreneurs, lawyers, pastors, teachers, professors, university deans, judges, MPs, and MPPs.

I graduated from the college in the spring of 1947 and started in the seminary that fall. The experience of change was minimal. The building, dormitory, classrooms, boarding club, even some faculty, remained the same. But classes were smaller—ours numbered only five, all male, mostly second career.

Courses were academically oriented, with, for example, emphasis on exegesis of scripture but little or no exegesis of society or the person. No courses were available in Christian education or pastoral counselling. The course in preaching included voice training! Summer parish supply work provided the major opportunity for practical experience. I was fortunate to have the opportunity of parish experience at St. Mark's, Kitchener, during the school year. Apparently I startled some of the St. Mark's members when in one of my Christmas sermons I mentioned that the Holy

Family was in a house when the Three Wise Men arrived and that, therefore, they and shepherds did not arrive simultaneously. But they didn't hold
it against me, because a few years later I received a call from St. Mark's to
be their pastor, which I had to decline in favour of graduate studies.

Parish emergencies in my first pastorate at New Dundee–Mannheim
(1950–56) came as a challenge. Parents' anxiety over the sudden death of
their unbaptized baby; a triple murder and suicide; a mentally disturbed
wife and mother disrupting a family; the drowning of a young husband
and father on a Sunday-morning fishing trip. These emergencies kept
me connected with the seminary for advice and support. But, more significantly, they indicated my need for advanced education in pastoral
care and counselling.

Scholarships and an unprecedented partly paid leave of absence provided by the parish launched me into a year of studies in pastoral counselling at Boston University School of Theology (1954–55). That master's
degree proved to be the springboard for my future at the college and
seminary.

My next pastoral call (1956–60) located me in Waterloo, where I developed and organized Mount Zion Lutheran Church. Dr. Ulrich Leupold,
the seminary's academic dean, was the organist at the church. Alongside
pastoral duties I was also lecturing part-time at the seminary. In addition,
the Lutheran regional body that oversaw the seminary elected me to the
college and seminary Board of Governors. As chair of the board I was
extensively involved in negotiations between St. Jerome's and Waterloo
colleges and the proposed University of Waterloo as well as the severing
of Waterloo College's relationship with the University of Western Ontario.
The result was Waterloo Lutheran University with a degree-granting
charter. This took place in 1959 through an act of the Ontario legislature, with my name as one of the signatories.

In 1960 I resigned from the Board of Governors to accept a call to
the seminary faculty as assistant professor of Practical Theology. This
appointment in effect created the seminary's first department of practical theology, which included preaching, teaching, and pastoral care and
counselling and, later, also internship and clinical training. I also served
as dean of the chapel. In 1963 I was assigned the task of arranging the dedication ceremony of the new seminary building. Due to prohibitive repair
costs, Willison Hall was demolished soon after.

The campus unrest of the sixties showed up in the seminary before it did in the university It was initiated by a group of seminarians who called themselves the Fiery Furnace Five. The seminary faculty turned to the professor of Practical Theology for guidance. In my clinical program at Boston University I had experienced a method called group dynamics, also known as group process or sensitivity training. With the faculty's consent I engaged four certified trainers from our Lutheran partners in the US. For one week all classes were cancelled. Students, faculty, and administrators gathered in plenary or group sessions that included both verbal and non-verbal communication and the expression both of ideas and of feelings.

At mid-week one of the faculty said to me, "Glebe, what damn Pandora's box have we opened up!" But by week's end transformation had occurred. The faculty lounge was open to all. Faculty and students were on a first-name basis. Teaching methods became more student-inclusive. A sense of community and collegiality began to develop. The seminary's way of "living and learning and having its being" had changed drastically and permanently. The challenge now was how to convey to the parishioners who supported the seminary and to the general public that the seminary had not become a haven for hippies!

The Canadian Association of Pastoral Education (CAPE), founded in 1965, had a significant impact upon our seminary curriculum. The clinical emphasis of CAPE led to adding to the seminary curriculum a quarter (three months) of pastoral experience in a hospital setting under a CAPE-certified supervisor. A year of internship in a parish or hospital also became part of the requirements for graduation. The Interfaith Pastoral Counselling Centre established in Kitchener in 1967 also had a deep and long-lasting effect upon enrolments, programs, and staffing at the seminary. I was a charter member of CAPE, president in 1970, and chair of the accreditation and certification committee for many years. The committee accredited all clinical programs and certified all members across Canada. The position enabled our seminary to have close contact with theological developments in Canada.

In 1970 I graduated from Knox College, Toronto School of Theology, with my doctoral degree in pastoral counselling. In that same year Dean Leupold, the administrative head of the seminary (1968–70), died suddenly. I was appointed principal-dean (a new title) of the seminary by the

Waterloo Lutheran University Board of Governors, a position in which I continued until 1984, when at age sixty-five I retired from administration.

During my tenure of office the seminary was involved in two major relationships. One was with the Kitchener–Waterloo Interfaith Pastoral Counselling Centre mentioned earlier. The centre developed two counselling streams. The one, focused on chaplaincy and pastoral counselling, was accredited by CAPE. The other stream, marriage and family counselling, focused on issues in the context of family and was accredited by the American Association for Marriage and Family Therapy. As principal-dean of the seminary, I participated in accreditation procedures. I also served as a member of the centre's Board of Governors and as chair of the professional advisory committee. Conversely, some of the centre's teaching staff also taught courses for the seminary. Aarne Siirala, the seminary's professor of theology, taught courses in theology and therapy, but the entire faculty was involved in teaching counselling students. A spirit of trust and cooperation made the relationship beneficial and meaningful for both the seminary and the centre.

The seminary's other major relationship was with the university and, after 1973, with the university's religious studies faculty in what was called the School of Religion and Culture (SORAC). Some religious studies and seminary courses were cross-listed in the respective calendars and taught by faculty from whichever of the two institutions actually offered the particular courses.

Having recently completed my doctoral thesis on the subject of grief (1970), at the suggestion of a SORAC faculty member I began to offer courses on aging and change, death and dying, and current ethical issues at the undergraduate level—to a surprising overflow of students. I offered the same topics at the graduate level to both seminary and social work students. The resulting income from these courses was good news for a tight seminary budget.

These arrangements were made possible by attending to my seminary administration duties in the daytime and teaching the undergraduate courses in the evenings. Much credit for this arrangement goes to my secretaries, Mavis Lewin and later Bette Smith, for managing the seminary office so competently.

With the increased seminary enrolments and expansion of the number of courses, the need emerged for the creation or modification of degree programs. The Master of Divinity (M.Div.) prepared for pastoral ministry; we increased the program to four years to include an additional year of internship in a parish as well as three months of clinical training. An M.Div.–M.A. program was created in cooperation with SORAC and an M.Div.–M.S.W. program in cooperation with the School of Social Work. The Master of Theological Studies (M.T.S.) prepared for qualification for AAMFT or CAPE certification. The Master of Theology (M.Th.) in pastoral counselling was a two-year program that would follow upon completion of one of the other master's programs. Under my successors Dr. Richard Crossman and Dr. David Pfrimmer, a doctoral program in counselling was added as well.

A signal event during this same period was the ordination for parish ministry (1976) of the seminary's first woman graduate, Pamela McGee. A very significant number of other women followed in her steps. This development not only increased enrolments but also significantly changed the content and conduct of seminary courses and affected the ethos of the seminary community and of the churches where they exercised their ministries.

In 1982 the accreditation team from the Association of Theological Schools in the US and Canada visited and assessed the seminary and granted it full accreditation—a first for the seminary. The student body by this time included not only Canadian Lutherans but also Anglicans, United Church members, Roman Catholics, Baptists, Mennonites, and Mormons as well as students from the US, Guyana, and Africa. The chair of the accreditation committee commented, "You are ecumenical in your program and practice and yet have retained your Lutheran identity."

In 1986 the regional church body that oversaw the seminary merged with another Lutheran church body to create a specifically Canadian Lutheran church body, the Evangelical Lutheran Church in Canada. For the seminary the merger meant separation from the rich resources of our former church body, the Lutheran Church in America, and a major reorientation, with both loss and gain.

By 1984 I had reached the age of sixty-five, a provincially mandated time of retirement. However, by annual renewal of contract I continued on the seminary faculty for another eighteen years. My contract, dated June 7, 1985, outlined my responsibilities: teach six one-term WLU undergraduate classes plus two one-term seminary classes; provide directed studies and theses supervision; attend faculty meetings; serve as director of the counselling program. As I looked at it, I realized that was what I had been doing during the past fourteen years, along with the duties of administration. Added to these in 1986 was chairing the two-million-dollar fund drive to celebrate the seminary's seventy-fifth anniversary. It meant travelling with the synodical bishop in a rented Chevrolet across Ontario, Quebec, and Nova Scotia. (It worked!)

At ninety-two years of age, and looking back upon those forty-two years, I am grateful for many honours and awards, including an honourary doctorate from WLU, the Delton Glebe Chair of Pastoral Counselling, the seminary alumni's Distinguished Graduate Award, and the WLU alumni's Hoffman-Little Award of Excellence. I also realized that during those forty-two years I had not had one paid sabbatical. Time passed so quickly I guess I hadn't noticed!

Chapter 5

An R.C. Comes to WLU: Early Days of Social Work and a Threefold Maturation Process

FRANK TURNER

THE OPENING OF THE GRADUATE SCHOOL OF SOCIAL WORK AT Waterloo Lutheran in 1966 was an historic event for the university, for the profession, and for me personally. Although at the time we did not realize it, in those heady early days we were all making history as we moved from a small church-related university to a full-fledged institution of higher education with a rich and strong profile of programs, faculty, and staff.

I had never looked back in an analytical way on my earliest days at WLU until Rose Blackmore invited me to contribute a chapter to this book. I had not realized that those early days of what quickly became known as the Faculty of Social Work were part of a process of institutional growth and maturation on many fronts that was at the same time a process of maturation, both academic and personal, for the seven or eight people who launched that process.

I came to Waterloo Lutheran in the early spring of 1966 as the first full-time faculty member in the newly established school following the appointment of Sheldon Rahn as dean a month earlier. I was (and still am) a Roman Catholic, at that time teaching in a Roman Catholic college of the University of Ottawa but coming now to a university that was very consciously Lutheran. Subsequent to my appointment, I was told that it was a matter of more than casual discussion at some early university board meetings that the first two appointments to the new school would be a Roman Catholic as professor and a Quaker as dean.

The opening of the school in the fall of 1966 came at a time when social work in Canadian universities was rapidly expanding. The mental health movement was a high priority of the federal government of the day. Thus there was federal money available to the universities to start or expand programs in social work at a graduate level. It was clear that another social work program was needed in this southwestern part of Ontario. Windsor was being talked about but had not yet taken any action. Waterloo Lutheran was in a growth mode; some even suggested that our becoming a public university in the future was a distinct possibility. Others thought this to be a foolish fantasy and an abandonment of the university's strong Lutheran tradition.

William Villaume, the Lutheran president of WLU, himself a social worker by training, saw the advantages of having a graduate school of social work at the university. Since his background was American, most of his social work contacts were American. He knew well an American named Sheldon Rahn, a graduate of Columbia with a reputation as an organizer, whom he thought he could lure to Canada if a school were established. It was fortunate that several factors were already in place. WLU, as a Lutheran university, had a strong commitment of service to the community as well as a firm commitment to higher education—social work accorded well with the mores of our institution. With the expansion of social work across the country that was taking place and with resources available for doing so, the addition of social work to the university made sense—a next logical step in an expanded WLU. Thus the Senate and Board of Governors voted in favour of the school.

Once the decision was made and an academic entity consisting of Sheldon, myself, and a multi-function staff person was in place, it was clear that we needed a home on campus. For a variety of reasons never fully explained to us, the newly emerging school was housed in the seminary. Difficult as I am sure that was for the seminary, Dean Leupold made us feel very welcome. (I sometimes think that it was more than convenience that our first home on the campus was in the seminary, where an eye could be kept on these two non-Lutheran faculty—who were social workers on top of it!)

However, the seminary faculty of the day welcomed us warmly and generously shared their academic resources with us. One of the first spinoffs of the association was the combined M.S.W.–M.Div. degree, a

program that is still in place. Indeed, on all sides we experienced enthusiasm and cooperation and a wide range of accommodation both formal
and informal. For example, in a very short period of time the library had
developed an excellent beginning collection for our new program.

Obviously a new program required a new curriculum, and in the
summer of 1966 the University of Toronto loaned us five of their senior
social work faculty, who drove weekly to Waterloo and met with us in the
seminary board room. Their mandate was to construct a new curriculum for us. This was an example of inter-university co-operation not to
be forgotten. I don't know whether those Toronto colleagues received an
honorarium or whether the Lutheran tradition of charity assumed that
this would be a pro bono contribution. As I got to know Sheldon and his
Quaker roots better, I began to suspect that there was no fee paid.

As all this was taking place, word of the new program was out and we
began to receive a large number of inquiries, informal applications, and
requests for admission, although we did not yet have a formal admission process. In fact, we had not as yet made a clear decision as to when
we would admit our first students, although the general assumption was
that it would be in September of 1967. However, the enthusiasm that had
been generated, the quality of persons seeking admission, and the support of the university were so marked we decided that we should not
wait another year. Once again the University of Toronto stepped forward
and the members of the curriculum committee became the admissions
committee and began a review of the cohort of informal applicants we
had received.

Given these various levels of support, the campus-wide enthusiasm
and support, the encouragement of our colleagues, and the quality of
senior colleagues that were coming forward to serve as faculty, the decision was made, with the approval of the Senate, not to wait until 1967 but
to admit our first class in September of 1966. (This was one area where
our Toronto colleagues had some reservations, in that they thought we
should wait a year.)

The formal opening of the school took place one evening in the fall
of 1966. It was indeed a glorious occasion, attended by a large number
of senior politicians, bureaucrats, academics, clergy, community social
workers, and representatives of other health professions as well as members of the general public.

As the school was developing on all fronts, the university was also progressing. New buildings were being constructed, new programs established, and faculty research was increasing markedly. A sense of excitement and expectancy pervaded the campus. One day we all came to our offices and lecture halls to learn that our maturation process had taken an important and historic step forward. No longer were we WLU, we were now ... WLU. The retention of the same initials for the new name was much more than the saving of a few dollars on football shirts. The new era built on our tradition as Waterloo Lutheran University. But, as Wilfrid Laurier, we had moved into the major league with a huge increase in our budget and a commitment to becoming a university of stature.

We were now riding pretty high with our new Graduate School of Social Work and a developing network of community partners within the Golden Triangle. We were also fulfilling our primary mandate of graduating classes of M.S.W. students who were beginning to assume senior positions in the network of social services in a wide array of settings. However, one event in the early life of our school tempered our euphoria in a most dramatic way. One morning, sitting in the dean's office, I received a call that two of our second-year students, John Easton and Chris McCarney, had just been killed in an automobile accident. We were a closely knit group at the school, young enough and small enough to be greatly shaken by the tragedy. It reminded us of the existential reality that growth and development take place in the reality of birth and death. Thus, as the school began as a young and fledging new component of WLU and matured institutionally, academically, and professionally, it also needed to acknowledge the reality of joy often tinged with sorrow that marks the world in which our graduates serve.

So here we are some forty-five years later. The school, renamed the Faculty of Social Work in 1974, has continued to mature, with new, more diverse and more inclusive programs and vision. It now occupies the beautifully renovated former St. Jerome's High School building on Duke Street in downtown Kitchener. The two-year M.S.W. program is still in place in addition to a very fine doctoral program. Much has changed, of course. Whatever has persisted reflects those exciting days of the mid-sixties when a prescient board, Senate, and synod took the decision that the then WLU could make an important contribution to the growth and development of Canada's social work network, first as WLU and then not long after as WLU.

Part Two

Getting Started

Chapter 6

From Two to Four and More— Early Days in Chemistry at WLU

RAY HELLER

$\mathcal{I}$N THE LATE 1950S, THE ONTARIO GOVERNMENT ENTERED INTO an arrangement to use Waterloo College, operated for many years by the Lutheran church, as the nucleus for the development of a full-spectrum provincially supported university. As part of this plan, something called the Associate Faculties was established to offer science and engineering programs. But the plan collapsed (with a certain degree of animosity among the administrators, I understand) and the Associate Faculties were transferred a short distance down University Avenue, there soon to become the University of Waterloo.

In 1960 Waterloo College became Waterloo Lutheran University, a largely liberal arts institution. In spite of continuing financial restrictions, efforts were soon under way to reestablish a science presence at the new university. In 1966, Dr. Mike Krech and I were hired as chemistry professors by Dr. Lloyd Schaus, the dean of Arts and Science. A fledgling chemistry department was already in operation offering a three-year general degree with a very limited number of courses taught by Chris Young and Kermit Way. Both of these gentlemen were scheduled to return to graduate school in the immediate future. I was fresh out of graduate school at the time, and when Dr. Schaus appointed me to be department chair I was rather flattered, even though no additional stipend was mentioned. Little did I appreciate the other duties (such as attendance at numerous meetings) that would go with the elevated position.

And more "other duties." Unlike any other academic chemistry department in Canada (in the world?), we had no technical support staff at all. This meant that, in addition to teaching courses, Mike and I had to assume responsibility for all non-classroom operations necessary for the functioning of the department. This included preparation of solutions, and the setting out and retrieving of those solutions, plus other chemicals and miscellaneous equipment needed in the student labs. As well, we were responsible for ordering all lab materials, glassware, instruments, and general equipment from science-supply companies and, upon their delivery, unpacking and shelving it all. This was, to put it mildly, quite time-consuming.

That particular problem was solved after a few years when President Frank Peters authorized the department to hire a part-time technician. That is how Alina Kinastowski came into our world. She was a recent immigrant, and communication was sometimes a problem, but she was intelligent, hard-working, and had a background in chemistry. We soon came to depend on her heavily, and before long she became a full-time employee of the department.

In 1969, Dr. Russell Rodrigo and Dr. John Kominar joined our department, a 100% increase in our faculty complement! We were thus able to offer more courses and to plan actively for one of our dreams: offering a four-year honours degree. During the next few years, our sister science departments were given honours programs (honours Computing in the Physics department, honours Biology), but the university administration, in their prudence, made chemistry wait many more years for the equivalent privilege, causing considerable frustration for the four faculty members.

Looking back, what impresses me is that, although we lacked a four-year honours program for so long, we were able to attract a reasonable number of excellent students over the years. We were very aware of the reality that, in addition to all the other chemistry departments in southern Ontario, we were competing with the rapidly growing reputation of the University of Waterloo, with its varied science, math, and engineering programs plus their seductive co-op option. It was sometimes a challenge to keep believing in our own department.

Throughout this entire period, the chemistry facilities were on the second floor of the central wing of the Arts Building. Our three very crowded labs had been converted from simple classrooms and were not at all properly designed or outfitted. Similarly, our chemical and equipment storerooms were incredibly cramped, probably violating safety regulations. And the main hallway, which we shared with the Biology department, was jammed with storage cabinets, refrigerators, and freezers. The low-quality water lines and drains in our renovated labs gave us problems for many years; we frequently caused aggravation when our plumbing broke down and floods of water poured through the ceilings of the classrooms on the first floor below us. We laboured under these conditions for too many years. But the fortunes of the department slowly improved. More faculty and additional support staff were hired. And, after years of having to share secretarial services with other departments, in 1991 we obtained our own full-time executive assistant, the dependable and well-organized Jane Gohl. With her cheery personality she soon became the face of chemistry at WLU.

Eventually, around 1992, the university informed us that funds had come available to finance a new science building, which would be constructed on the corner of King and Bricker streets. Those were exciting times for all the science personnel. Each department was allowed to work directly with the architects in designing the section of the building which they would occupy: labs for teaching and—wonder of wonders—for doing research, plus proper storage facilities and modern ventilation, hydro, and plumbing systems. As well, the structure had its aesthetic features, notably a large indoor courtyard with mature trees, open balcony-style hallways, and a high-level skylight. It would prove to be a pleasant environment for us.

Late summer of 1994: Moving Day. A very complicated operation, involving a rather vast array of equipment, chemicals, lab furniture, and general office contents. A commercial moving company had been engaged to carry everything out of the Arts Building, drive a couple of blocks across campus, and then, under the supervision of staff and faculty members, transfer it all into the new facilities

Deep in the basement, cavernous new storage areas were waiting to be filled. Some large glass bottles of powerful acids were transferred in heavy-duty cardboard boxes. Unfortunately, in the new storage bunker, some of those boxes had been stacked on top of each other, an arrangement for which they were not designed.

Very late that afternoon when almost everyone else had gone home for dinner, I went down to the basement storage area as part of my final savouring of the first day of our dream-come-true. Big trouble! Suffocating fumes in the hallways! The proper and prudent thing to do would have been to get out of there immediately, but I held my breath and took a quick peek which revealed that some of the improperly stacked cardboard boxes had collapsed and the acid bottles had shattered on the concrete floor. It was a mess which we were not equipped to deal with. So, in minutes, we had the Waterloo Fire Department and the Region of Waterloo hazardous waste personnel on the scene. In their astronaut-style suits and masks, they cleaned up our spill in a couple of hours and ventilated the basement hallways, thus serving as midwives to our unforgettable initial occupation of the chemistry section of the New Science Building.

With that unpleasant episode behind us, our needs and our hopes were wonderfully fulfilled by the new facility. And we all lived happily ever after!

Chapter 7

The Best Job I Ever Had

RALPH BLACKMORE

Before coming to WLU Ralph served in the RCAF during World War II, was financial editor of The Globe and Mail, *and worked in public relations for Massey Ferguson.*

The following is based on excerpts from a recording of an interview conducted by John McCutcheon in 1995 for the School of Business and Economics oral-history project. The recordings are deposited in the WLU Library archives. Frank Millerd transcribed and edited the interview. Ralph died in 2002.

Q. When did you come to Laurier?

A. In 1966, I came from Toronto. I was with the Massey Ferguson people there.

Q. What attracted you to Laurier?

A. I had always wanted to be a teacher at the university level and I always seemed to get turned off for one reason or another. I had a chance meeting with Herman Overgaard. I was in Niagara Falls doing a piece for a magazine I wrote for in New York. As a former newsman I had enough sense to look over the names of the people attending and it had Herman Overgaard, president of the university [Overgaard was actually chair of the Department of Business and Economics]. I immediately decided to cultivate Herman, which I did, and we got along fine. I wrote him a letter asking about a job. Herman wrote back and said there was a spot for me. Apparently someone had backed out of a job.

Q. What were your first impressions?

A. Well, to be honest, "Last Hope U." What have I done? Here I was and I had to go with it. It might have been Last Hope U, but it was such a nice friendly place. The first time I sat down to have lunch, Flora Roy, whom I love, was talking about the future of the university and said this just might be the last year. I thought, "What have I done?" I gave up a really well-paying job to come to a place that was going to die in three months. That was thirty years ago and it didn't happen.

Q. What was your first year like?

A. It was terrible. I was about one page ahead of the students. With a shortage of faculty in those days, you had to cover the waterfront. I had to teach a course on current Canadian economic problems. My immediate reaction was that I was going to have some of those economic problems myself before not too long. I got very cunning, necessary to stay alive. I said I want all you people to be in teams of two and I will write down a list of economic problems and each team will take one of these and you will present your paper at the next class. So I didn't have to do anything except sit there and listen to their reports…. It was a battle to stay alive but I loved it and I survived.

Those of us who taught tried to be imaginative and not just stay with the textbook. In a business class we talked about the stock market, so I thought it would be a good idea to put together a contest. I said that you all have $100,000 on such and such a day and you trade this $100,000 and by Christmas whoever has made the most money will get some money as a prize.

I found out I had a group of pretty resourceful students. I would get their reports at the end of each week and some of these people made $250,000—and I thought they should be teaching and I should be listening. Then I watched what they were doing. They would look at the paper and see the opening price of the stock was twenty-five cents and during the day went up to seventy-five cents. Then they would say that they had bought 100,000 shares at twenty-five cents and sold at seventy-five cents on the same day. They were always dealing in these kinds of stocks. Right off the bat I had to cancel the whole thing and start off again. Every week I had to stop something and start again. But it worked out after a while and got to be very smooth.

The idea spread and was copied by other universities. Tens of thousands have played the game and many are still playing. I think it is in fifty high schools across Ontario. It has been a tremendous success. I have had students come up to me since and say they learned a great deal about the stock market. By the time I had it perfected there was nothing they could do that was illegal. It has been great. I hope it goes on forever, very educational and useful.

It has had support from the business community. I promised to get some money for prizes and, having been financial editor of *The Globe and Mail* for a number of years, I knew people who did have money. So naturally I tapped them. One was Charlie Burns, who was the head of Burns Brothers and Denton. I think I asked him for $100 and he sent $500. I had no problem in raising the money. People were very, very generous. The whole thing just rolled along.

Q. Your most vivid memories?

A. A lot of people stand out. John Weir for one, one of the ablest men I have ever met—and I have known a few in my day. Able, helpful guy; nobody's pushover but a fine, fine guy.

A man I loved is a man called Klaus Bongart, a German guy, at least as tall as the Statue of Liberty, great big guy. He fought in the war and we met at one of the events they held in September. I bumped into him and I turned around and I am looking straight at a belt buckle. I looked up and thought, I hope he likes me. He was a German and I asked if he was in the war. He replied, yeah, he was in the war. On the wrong side, I was sure of that. I said: "What did you do in the war?" He said he was anti-aircraft. I said, "You big so-and-so"—and that I was in the air force. He said, "The war is over." On that basis we built a friendship that just got bigger and bigger.

Q. Did you make the right decision to come?

A. Absolutely, never had a doubt. It was such a friendly, happy little place and everybody loved it. It was just great. I don't think I ever met an unfriendly person the whole faculty. As the university gets larger it will be a sorry thing if the cozy feeling goes. It's better than it was. It's more professional than it was. It's got more experts. The experts pretty much make the students toe the line. Last Chance U was a thousand years ago.

I will tell you how good I now think the school is. I want my grandchildren to come here. If I have to let them live with me for free I will even make that sacrifice.

Chapter 8

Spatial Memories, Mostly Geographical, Mostly of the Sixties and Seventies

HERBERT A. WHITNEY

I BEGAN TEACHING AT WATERLOO LUTHERAN UNIVERSITY IN THE Department of Geography, Geology, and Planning in September of 1965. I'd been interviewed by the department chair, John McMurry, at the annual meeting of the American Association of Geographers in the spring of the year, then came to Waterloo, where I met with Dean Lloyd Schaus and President William Villaume. I parked where the Dr. Alvin Woods Building now stands. Along Albert Street was a row of modest houses, one of which, I believe, housed the English department. The Geography department was on the third floor of the new east wing of the main building on University Avenue.

McMurry was rebuilding the Geography department, the older one having moved down the road to the University of Waterloo in 1962. I never felt animosity between the two departments; mostly, we just went our separate ways. The split between UW and WLU was old history as far as I was concerned.

Most attractive to me was the size of Waterloo Lutheran University, about 1,800 students at the time. My wife and I both had undergraduate degrees from small liberal arts colleges and preferred them to large universities. In addition, WLU had a geography department larger than any in any similar-size college I knew of—an ideal combination!

One of the good things about a small school is that faculty get to know each other regardless of their departments. This was fostered during my first two years at WLU by a September weekend retreat at Jordan

Harbour for all faculty. I remember being impressed by the report given
by Duncan MacLulich, head of the Biology department, on the research
he was doing. Later, Flora Roy, head of the English department, snagged
me to be the first chair of the newly created Cultural Affairs committee;
so then I worked closely with Walter Kemp, head of the Music department, and his secretary Carol Raymond. Faculty Wives was an active
organization. They organized an annual kids' Christmas party, with John
Weir as Santa. Through informal gatherings such as these I got to know
faculty in other departments better: Bob Fisher, Religious Studies; Jim
Harkins, History; Bob Langen, Philosophy; Bob McCauley, Biology; Kurt
Nabert, German; Charles Paape, History; Ed Riegert, Seminary; Don
Morgenson, Psychology; Terry Scully, French.

The Geography faculty when I arrived consisted of Lorne Russwurm,
Ken Kelly, Stuart Harris, and Harold Keuper, who soon left to work on
his advanced degree; they handled all the geology and physical geography courses. Lorne, Ken, Stuart, and I had Ph.D.s and together with John
McMurry initiated a graduate program in geography. Thereafter, only
faculty with Ph.D.s were tenured.

During the summer just before arriving, I had spent six weeks at Ohio
State University for a course in quantitative geography, which was just
making inroads into the more traditional descriptive geography. So I was
the first quantitative geographer in our department and hastened to
include chi-square in an introductory geography lab exercise, explaining
it to the lab instructors and fielding student complaints. As the department
grew and more experts arrived, I shed some of my original courses.

The chair shared his office with the department secretary, Lillian
Peirce, who before retiring in 1984 typed all our course outlines, tests,
exams, department meeting minutes, reports, etc. George Priddle arrived
when I did, and our first "office" consisted of two desks in the large map
room adjacent to the chair's office. Large filing cases held large, flat draw-
ers full of maps. Closets along the walls held huge rolled-up wall maps
that were taken to classrooms and then back, the classrooms being used
by other departments as well. (I remember teaching in a small room in
the main building. When the door opened, the student seated behind it
got hidden.) At either end of our third-floor hall were the geography
and geology labs. In those early years, calculators and instruments were
left out even overnight for students to use. The stairs at the south end led

to both the Torque Room and the faculty lounge, where faculty of all the departments ate and conversed and watched the president's house being built. It had a room for the chancellor to use when on campus.

Between the faculty lounge and the president's house, where the Fred Nichols Centre is now located, was a playing field. Some people thought that the view up across the playing field should be topped by a chapel, not the squat new two-storey library. Down on King Street, where the Athletic Complex now stands, was a cider mill. Remnants of its orchard, three apple trees, may still exist on the south side of Clara Conrad Residence.

WLU's main building with its new east wing was a combination of departments and administration and service offices. Geography shared the third floor with Biology, beyond which was the large room (over the main-floor entrance lobby) where faculty association meetings were held. Beyond the main-floor entrance lobby were the offices of the registrar, finance officer, dean, and president. Along the basement hallway were small rooms, used by Physics, as I recall, and at the western end was the print shop with cubbyholes for mail at the front. I remember the spring all-faculty meetings in 1E1 to discuss student marks; if a student was a little shy of graduating, could someone raise a mark a bit?

Field trips were a traditional, inherent part of geography courses, with a week-long field camp required of third-year geography honours students so they could gain familiarity with field techniques such as surveying, plane tabling across varied terrain, and reading the glaciated landscape. Where to hold the camp? After classes ended in April 1966, John McMurry and I, along with George Priddle, who was familiar with Algonquin Park, scouted out the park as a possible site. Near Lake of Two Rivers we found the Wildlife Research Station. It was busy during the warmer seasons but down to skeleton staff in the fall. It became our field camp base that fall and for half a dozen years thereafter.

Because field camp was the last week of September, we got our classes quickly under way and filled lab instructors in on their duties while all the faculty would be away at camp. An all-male faculty meant that wives were left at home with young kids for six days. On Monday at 6 a.m. faculty and students assembled at the university parking lot with all our gear ready to be stowed in the vans that faculty had rented the day before. We travelled in convoy, checking that the following van hadn't had trouble. Our route was around Guelph, through Erin and Alliston, with an 8 a.m. coffee stop at the McDonalds at Highway 400, which had been built that far by then. Then on to Algonquin, noting en route the sign at the site of WLU's proposed Orillia campus. At the Wildlife Research Station an experienced lumber camp cook had a hearty lunch awaiting us, after which the daily routine was established with times for meals, cabin assignments, and field work plans.

Students on KP had to be at the kitchen at 6 a.m. to get everything ready both for breakfast and for all of us who had to make our brown-bag lunches, and then to get everything washed and cleaned up by 9 a.m., when the cook left until mid-afternoon and our vans departed for their different projects. My project usually was vegetative sampling (which *The Cord* once reported as "vegetable sampling"). It involved dividing my group into trios, stationed 250 feet apart at the highway. Each trio then followed the same compass direction and every 250 feet stopped and recorded the vegetation within a ten-foot radius. Later we combined the field notes into comprehensive maps showing distribution and density of different species.

Evenings were spent all together in the dining room, faculty answering questions as students wrote up the day's field notes. Faculty and students got to know each other informally. With no TVs or electronic devices, we had to provide our own entertainment—bridge, poker, or chess, or maybe a student on guitar or fiddle. Some beer, yes, but no boozing—we had work to do the next day.

Saturday morning, the last day, followed the usual breakfast routine, but then we had to load all our gear and equipment and clean the cabins, finally getting away mid-morning, travelling in convoy again, eating our brown-bag lunches en route, and arriving back in Waterloo mid-afternoon. Usually that weekend or the next was Homecoming, for which the Geography Club made a float for the parade down King Street.

One particular incident sticks in my mind. The research at the Wildlife Centre involved wolves, and there were two pens of them. They often howled at night. One time a student from bustling, bright, noisy Hong Kong was picked up at the airport and brought to camp. When she awoke that first evening after a nap there was no one around at the neighbouring cabins, the woods were dark, and wolves were howling—imagine the culture shock! Apparently she'd missed a dinner announcement of a get-together at the cabin on the rise across the creek. Fortunately she was missed and someone came and rescued her.

After the Algonquin years we went other places: the Huntsman Marine Lab in New Brunswick, Moosonee, Manitoulin Island, Stony Lake, and Petawawa Forest Station. When the urban and economic geography faculty members complained that the field techniques didn't serve their needs, we went to Quebec City (six times), Montreal, Ottawa, and Collingwood. The field trip in 1991 to Haileybury/New Liskeard was my last.

Over the years, faculty came and went, especially at first. But there was also marked stability: the faculty in 1976—John McMurry, Gunars Subins, Jerry Hall, Ian McKay, Russell Muncaster, Alfred Hecht, Bruce Young, Grant Head, Barry Boots, Houston Saunderson, Helen Parson, Ken Hewitt—were all still there (plus four more) when I retired in 1993. It was a pleasure to work with each of these good people. I taught at WLU for twenty-eight years, Helen for twenty-six years, but we are both outdone by Ian at thirty-three years.

I'll conclude with one dislike and two likes I've had. Early departmental meetings were in a small room and several faculty members smoked; I disliked the smoke. In the university faculty meetings people smoked, too. Fortunately, the university instituted a no-smoking policy. What I particularly liked about the Geography department over the years was its collegiality. Faculty members genuinely liked each other; the field camps/trips played a large part in that. Retired members now get together monthly for lunch, and field trips commonly get mentioned. I liked, too, the open-door policy, also initiated by John McMurry; students felt welcome to stop in and ask questions or to just chat. There was always good rapport between faculty and students. It was a great time to be at WLU!

Chapter 9

In the Beginning: Life at Biology— and Off Campus

ROBERT W. McCAULEY

I CAME TO WATERLOO LUTHERAN UNIVERSITY AND THE BIOLOGY department in 1965. The department was founded by Dr. Duncan MacLulich, famous for his discovery of cycles in the size of animal populations. In those days we were affiliated with the Lutheran church and received only federal operating grants, which meant money was tight. Duncan was the right man to nurture biology at the young university because of his skilful planning and his ingenuity in making do with limited resources. For example, space was limited and we followed a principle with a long history in which rooms are used for different purposes depending on the time of day. Thus the larger of the two teaching laboratories served as the venue for the first-year introductory course and was attended, in shifts, by hundreds of students.

The smaller lab accommodated a number of senior courses, depending on the week and the time of day. Courses included histology and embryology taught by Dr. Kay Hayashida, genetics and plant taxonomy (Dr. Arnold Wellwood), animal taxonomy and ecology (Dr. MacLulich), vertebrate anatomy (Dr. Edward Kott), and animal physiology, which I taught. The logistics of the department and its housekeeping were ably handled by our factotum in the person of technician John Szierer.

Duncan was a gadgeteer and his office, which he shared with Arnold Wellwood and resembled the interior of a submarine, was stuffed with equipment. However, Arnold soon moved discreetly to stake his claim to

46

the herbarium, which housed the collection of dried vascular plants—
an enclave in the geography wing coveted by that department.

Things are not always what they seem, also in the Biology department
back then. An embarrassing incident occurred resulting from our ingenious approach to coping with limited facilities. Today the department has
a proper refrigerated cold room in which to keep cold-blooded vertebrates
such as frogs. But in the early days we were forced to improvise. We kept
the amphibians in a modified refrigerated soft-drink cooler in the corridor
on the second floor of the Arts and Science building not far from the then
chapel, which also served at the time as the university senate chamber. We
had neglected to paint over the beckoning red-and-white Coca-Cola logo
on its sides. And one evening the cover was left unlocked. On that fateful
evening, when the senate session was over, the door of the senate chamber
burst open and a thirsty George Durst spotted the enticing (and unlocked)
cooler. His eyes lit up, he made a beeline to the cooler, lifted the cover in
search of "the pause that refreshes" and beheld instead a jumble of leaping
amphibians. He quickly closed the lid, his face registering a simultaneous
mixture of surprise, horror, and disgust. That he recovered from this psychological trauma was evident at lunchtime in the faculty lounge the next
day where he was his old jovial and slightly outrageous self.

One thing I learned in my years in the department was that sometimes
a little "incentive" works. When I taught a course in fish biology I would
bring the class to a fish hatchery to show students the life cycle of rainbow
trout from egg to adult. Tours of government trout-rearing stations were
welcome, since personnel wished to show taxpayers the importance of fish
hatcheries in maintaining fish populations. One time I approached the
operator of a nearby private hatchery to enquire about the possibility of
arranging a tour. His response was negative, and slightly hostile. "I don't
have time to show school classes about the hatchery. I am the only person
carrying out the chores necessary to running this operation. These include
feeding fish and cleaning screens and the rearing troughs." He added that
teachers "are always asking for guided tours. They don't realize how busy
I am." As a former hatchery biologist for the province I understood the
work involved in rearing fish and was sympathetic to his plight.

"Would you consider being a guest lecturer for an hour for an honorarium of $50?" I asked.

"Sure," he replied. "When are you coming?"

Chaucer observed that when April's sweet showers had pierced to the root the drought of March, people longed to go on pilgrimages. When spring came to WLU and classes were over, we looked forward to Gerry Noonan's one-day excursion around the region which he dubbed the Faculty Tour—understood as the Faculty *Cultural* Tour. He drew up a whimsical itinerary of the points of interest and the country public houses. Because of frequent stops to slake our thirst, cynics referred to our pilgrimage wanderings as a "pub crawl." (Those were the days when the title "designated driver" did not exist.) On one of these educational explorations we rented a yellow school bus and visited the African Lion Safari in Freelton where the wardens screamed at us to keep the windows closed. It was on this excursion that Duncan MacLulich showed us the scratches on the outcrop of bedrock on the side of Highway 6 caused by the last glacier. It was a cultural tour after all!

These tours opened our eyes to the interesting sites within an hour's driving distance from the campus: stone houses in Paris; the Elora Gorge; the Cockshut mansion, where we stopped for tea; fresh-caught hatchery trout cooked by Edna Staebler; the Queen's hotel in Ayr, where we challenged the locals at shuffleboard; vintage country pubs. Sadly, attendance dropped off over the years as participants became less concerned about *education* and more preoccupied with their end-of-term duties.

Gerry once told a story about himself that one could title *Share and Share Alike*. He had irregular eating habits, which confounded us since he ate meals at all hours. He especially liked desserts. Since he ran several miles a day, the consumption of these sweets had no effect on his weight. One Friday afternoon he and three colleagues from the English department went to a local restaurant for coffee. His companions ordered coffee, but Gerry, feeling hunger pangs, ate three (expensive) desserts in succession. When the server presented the bill he absent-mindedly—and cavalierly—suggested it that it would be simplest to split the sum four ways. Surprisingly, his tablemates raised no objections. Later he shamefacedly realized that he had consumed the lion's share of the refreshments—and (I am sure) made it up to them.

An extraterrestial biologist doing research on fauna in Waterloo Region would surely include Gerry's Faculty Cultural Tours as part of the study. I know I would.

Chapter 10

Physics, Administration, Astronomy— and Music

ARTHUR READ

M Y VERY FIRST CONTACT WITH WLU CAME VIA RAY KOENIG. At the time I had no idea how much Ray would become part of my life or how much of my life would be devoted to Laurier; in fact, at the time of this writing that connection has yet to reach a natural conclusion.

I was completing a master's degree at McMaster University and while I was giving a pre-lab talk to second-year undergraduates Ray entered the lab and stood at the back waiting for me to finish my presentation. Ray, a graduate of McMaster himself, had brought some Waterloo Lutheran University students to McMaster to view the nuclear reactor and to see "physics in action." In talking with his former supervisor, he had mentioned me as someone who might be interested in teaching at a smaller institution like WLU. On Ray's invitation I came to WLU for a tour and before long found myself in the office of Dean Lloyd Schaus. Shortly thereafter President Bill Villaume asked Ray if he wanted to hire this "young lad," and I was offered the position. We haggled over a starting salary (how bold was I?) and I was hired. That is how it was done in 1966! As I tell this story, I think of how, some 20 years later, I found myself across the table from Doug Lorimer and other members of the Wilfrid Laurier University Faculty Association negotiating the first contract for full-time faculty and wondering how I would have made it through the appointment process that we were about to "set in stone" in the initial collective bargaining agreement.

How vividly I remember my very first university lecture. It was a second-year electricity and magnetism class in good old 2c8, starting at eight in the morning. Why eight? Because, as at least some will recall, WLU still had chapel time scheduled into the timetable (that was familiar to me already from McMaster) and classes had to start early to leave open a time slot for chapel. I was all of twenty-four years old, and I was nervous. Thank goodness that the students were still half asleep and that there was a long desk at the front of the lecture room so that they couldn't see my knees knocking!

It wasn't long before I realized how much I loved my "job." Our department was small, just three of us: Ray Koenig, John Keil, and I. But there were young, dynamic colleagues in Chemistry (Mike Krech and Ray Heller began the same year), Biology (I remember Duncan McLulich well and Bob MacCauley, with whom I later collaborated on a few research projects), and Math (who could forget Frank Sweet?). However, the university was small enough that I quickly got to know colleagues in Music, Business, English, History, and French (Joan Kilgour and I knew each other from the McMaster Glee Club). In fact, it wasn't long before everyone knew everyone else. But it wasn't just faculty members—it was staff as well. There was often little to distinguish staff from faculty—we were all there to do a job for "Last Chance U." We were one big happy family, and, yes, there were family quarrels!

Last Chance U! In the late 60s and early 70s that's how WLU was known in some circles. Students who couldn't get into any other university could (almost) always get into WLU. Easy to get into but hard to get out of (with a degree, of course)—that was our challenge. With terrific staff like Fred Nichols, Tuffy Knight, Rich Newbrough, Erich Schultz, Helene Forler, and faculty colleagues with great reputations like Don Morgenson, Flora Roy, Jane Campbell, John McMurray, and Karl Aun (to name a few), the university forged a new identity and our reputation began to grow. My friend and colleague Hart Bezner, whom I had known since our early McMaster days, was hired in 1967 based somewhat on my recommendation. Of course Hart, who came with a completed doctorate in physics, made a significant contribution to Laurier's development by pioneering Computing Services, which you can read about elsewhere in this book.

Anticipating that a doctoral degree was essential if I were to maintain my faculty status and apply for tenure someday, I headed down the street to the University of Waterloo to see if I could begin work on a Ph.D. WLU didn't push me to do this; in fact it wasn't even encouraged, but I could see the writing on the wall (and it wasn't graffiti!). I remember talking to one senior faculty member in the hall one day who asked me why I "was doing that" (i.e., working on a Ph.D.) and quietly advised me not to bother. However, once I was enrolled in the doctoral program I must say that the university totally supported me and by 1973 I had my degree in hand and tenure followed soon after.

The year 1973 was an important year in my life, but it was even more important in the life of WLU. The senior academics and administrators of the day, contemplating a future of half-grant funding, decided the situation was unsustainable. I remember President Frank Peters as the visionary who realized that the only way the university could survive was to convince the Bill Davis government that WLU ought to be a "provincial" university.

I remember Frank, the teacher, lecturing across the hall from my office in the E Wing. I would always leave my door open just enough to hear his booming voice and think what an inspiration he must be to those lucky students listening to him lecture. In those days most faculty shared office space, so both Hart Bezner and I were blessed with Frank's memorable tones. Interestingly, my wife, Caroline, had got to know Bill Davis when he was just getting into politics, since she used to babysit the Davis children when she was a teen growing up in Brampton (which is where she and I met). So, in the fall of 1973, WLU changed its name to WLU. Many felt the new name was contrived so that the big red WLU letters on the Arts Building wouldn't have to be changed! Personally I thought it was a stroke of genius. Now Sir Wilfrid Laurier is justly honoured by his namesake, which has become known across the country and justifiably recognized as an important entity in post-secondary education in Canada.

The Physics, Chemistry, and Biology departments occupied the C Wing of the Arts Building and with the growing interest in science education it became clear that our lab facilities were inadequate. The Physics department took over the Torque Room (the room below 2c8). It seemed appropriate that Physics would eventually have the Torque Room for its use, *torque* being a physics term for a turning force—so named (I was told by Ray Koenig) by science and engineering students

at the soon-to-be University of Waterloo. It even accommodated the university mailroom for a number of years before there was an on-campus
mail delivery service. As a consequence, it was a great meeting place for
faculty and staff. It was clear that the university was in desperate need of
better science facilities, but we had to wait twenty years to get what we
really needed. Much of the credit for the funding of the New Science
Building must go to President John Weir.

In the early 1970s the Music department asked the Physics department to offer a course in musical acoustics. Walter Kemp and Victor
Martens pressed the need upon us, but no one in our small department
felt qualified to develop such a course. Eventually I stepped forward
(reluctantly) and offered to give it a shot. All music students were required
to take "my" course and I quickly developed a rapport with the growing
Music department, which made me feel like an adjunct faculty member.
Teaching such a talented array of students was a highlight of my classroom experience and I certainly learned as much from them as they did
from me. I taught the course for over twenty-five years and have fond
memories of many students who still reconnect with me, a number of
them now regular members of the Kitchener-Waterloo Symphony.

The summer of 1978 brought a dramatic change in the personnel of
the senior administration. Norman Wagner, a pivotal academic in Laurier's history, was chosen to become the next vice-president: academic.
But the University of Calgary also had their eye on Norm and, at the
proverbial eleventh hour, convinced him to become their next president
(a wise choice, as the University of Calgary made great strides under his
leadership). John Weir was appointed vice-president: academic and, in
1982, president, with Max Stewart as acting vice-president: academic.
The following summer Russell Muncaster, dean of Arts and Science, was
named as acting vice-president: academic and Russell asked me to be
acting dean for a year. He gave me twenty-four hours to respond! I was
shocked but honoured. Where did this come from, and why me? Caroline, my dear spouse (and best friend), convinced me that I should accept
the challenge and was up for the job (so I can blame her for what followed!). The following year both Russell and I were appointed to full
five-year terms, so the "acting" part was removed from the title and we
dug in to do everything we could for Laurier. I enjoyed working with
Russell; he was a terrific vice-president: academic with a good vision for

Laurier. I was disappointed when he did not seek another term after his six-year stint in the position.

One of many highlights of my years as dean was my involvement in the annual faculty/staff musical presentations, the brainchild of Leslie O'Dell of the English department. One of Leslie's mandates was to bring theatre back to the Laurier campus. Along with talented faculty and students of the Faculty of Music many of us would devote many summer hours preparing for such presentations as *Camelot, South Pacific, Guys and Dolls,* and even Stephen's Sondheim's very challenging *Into the Woods.* Many of us took on major roles in these productions. I remember Glenn Carroll as Nicely Nicely Johnson in *Guys and Dolls,* Russell Muncaster as my tough gambling partner in that production, John Peters in some erudite role, Fred Nichols in a variety of roles, and Jim Wilgar, who always seemed to get roles where he wore a uniform. Even John Weir was once given a cameo role.

In the late 1980s the full-time faculty organized as a union designated Wilfrid Laurier University Faculty Association (WLUFA) and sought a collective bargaining agreement. The university team consisted of Reg Haney, Russell Muncaster, Shankar Yelaja (dean of Social Work), me, and various others brought in for specific articles. Of course, President John Weir and Vice-President: Finance Andy Berczi were important background players. Russell Muncaster decided to return to faculty ranks in the spring of 1989. Shankar Yelaja died unexpectedly. Suddenly it was essentially Reg and I, along with Earl Rayner, who kept track of important details of the negotiations.

WLUFA, to their credit, wanted the Cadillac version of an agreement, but the university had no taste for that. The negotiations were a long-drawn-out affair and I remember many "admin-side" huddles in my office, which was close to the dean's boardroom, where most of the negotiating took place. Eventually the two sides came to an agreement, partly with the help of a provincial mediator, and Reg and I got our lives back, as did our WLUFA colleagues. In the meantime, Donald Baker had been hired as vice-president: academic and Don became heavily involved in the next round of negotiations, which seemed to come up pretty quickly. Don and his wonderful wife, Heather, have remained good friends with us and we have visited them in the United Arab Emirates, where Don is currently the dean of Humanities and Social Sciences at the United Arab

Emirates University. He is still hale and hearty in his mid-seventies and has just published a history of Mount Royal College in Calgary, where he was president for nine years prior to coming to Laurier.

In the late 1990s Laurier was approached by the City of Brantford to consider an offer to develop a satellite campus. President Bob Rosehart consulted with respected colleagues Terry Copp and Arthur Stephen, among others, and soon they were off to look at potential facilities. Brantford was not in good shape. The downtown core had deteriorated, the general populace had a poor image of the city, and the provincial government appeared unconcerned about the city's dwindling fortunes. The city faithful believed they had been shunned when the provincial government was "handing out universities" and felt that a university presence was desperately needed. The city council, headed by a young mayor, Chris Friel, was determined to turn things around. I became involved when Terry Copp and Arthur Stephen recommended that I might be the right person to work on the development of a Laurier Brantford campus. When I was approached I was again surprised to be asked but considered it an interesting and unique challenge. After consulting with Vice-President: Academic Rowland Smith, I agreed to the appointment and left my fifteen years as the dean of Arts and Science to begin a new adventure.

I spent two years at the Brantford campus. The first year involved planning and developing the physical space (the Carnegie Library building in downtown Brantford), planning the curriculum (in collaboration with Rowland Smith), hiring the first full-time faculty for the campus (Peter Farrugia and Gary Warrick), and fostering an awareness of the campus throughout Ontario—all with great hopes of attracting eager students to the city. There were great people to work with in Brantford and the campus would not be the success it is today without the commitment of the city and the Grand Valley Educational Society, a group of talented and tireless influential citizens. One year later, in September 1999, we started classes for thirty-nine full-time and over 100 part-time students. Today the campus is a hive of academic activity for over 100 faculty and staff and about 2,500 full-time students enrolled in a variety of interesting programs.

By the end of that first academic year, I realized I had been in university administration for seventeen years (not counting my seven years as department chair) and that the daily commute to Brantford was taking precious time away from my personal life—and I missed my first love, which was being in the classroom. I resigned as dean of the Brantford campus, took my administrative leave, and returned to full-time teaching in the new Faculty of Science and the growing Department of Physics and Computer Science. At first, Doug Witmer took over on an interim basis in Brantford. I was delighted when Leo Groarke agreed to take my position at Laurier Brantford. Leo, a distinguished professor of philosophy at WLU, came to university administration reluctantly but did an amazing job of transforming Laurier Brantford into a vibrant and significant part of the Laurier culture.

During my leave it was determined that I would take over the teaching of the only astronomy course offered by Laurier. Ray Koenig was still teaching the course, in his retirement, but it was apparent that he was not in good health. Nora Znotinas, the department chair, asked me to teach the course but was worried (I learned later) that I would not be interested in taking on such an onerous task so late in my academic career. I had always had a latent interest in astronomy but had never studied the area in depth. It was an interesting challenge and has become a passion—a field I thoroughly enjoy. I still teach astronomy, now two one-term online courses. In fact, together with Shohini Ghose, a talented and dedicated member in our department, and a colleague at the University of Winnipeg, I have become involved in creating a Canadian version of an introductory astronomy textbook appropriately entitled *ASTRO*.

Laurier has been a tremendously significant part of my life. From a small outpost of the University of Western Ontario in the first half of the twentieth century, WLU slowly and artfully crafted its niche, growing from a small church-affiliated university into a widely recognized, medium-sized university with an enviable reputation. I am happy and proud to have been a small part of the exciting development of this outstanding university built with pride and dedication by so many.

Chapter 11

Community Psychology, Community Building, and Social Justice

ED BENNETT

Y PROFESSIONAL IDENTITY IS AS A COMMUNITY PSYCHOLOGIST. In the wider context, I have been a social justice worker in the classroom and community for almost five decades. I have worked to improve transactions between people and their environments and to promote community well-being.

Values have been at the heart of the work in community psychology and social intervention in which I have been involved over the decades. Our Canadian society and our world have created many problems by viewing and treating some people and societies as less than human. My work since the early sixties has been predicated on the inherent worth and dignity of every person and has been rooted in justice, equity, and compassion in human relations. The increasingly shared appreciation of these principles has been life-changing for many people in Canada and in the world community. Nevertheless, there are many challenges that we face in our efforts to build a sustainable Canadian and world community marked by peace, justice, and liberty for all. Given these values, I found WLU to have been a remarkable professional home for me. From the outset the university administration and the Psychology department provided the space and the support that enabled me to become meaningfully engaged with students and the community in social-justice efforts and in work in community capacity-building

Upon my arrival in 1971 the university supported my interest in developing a course on the psychology of exceptional children, youth, and adults—this at a time when such courses were rare in Canadian universities. During the seventies the course was also offered in the WLU extension program to hundreds of teachers and administrators from the Waterloo Region Board of Education who appreciated the applicability of the course content and processes to their work. At the request of the extension students, I also offered a "special topics" course titled "Educational Practicum for Teachers."

In 1971 the Psychology department supported my interest in creating the first course in community psychology at WLU with a group of nine students. It focused on a comprehensive health-planning project in a three-county rural Appalachian area in southeast Ohio. I had a $10,000 contract to work as a consultant with the three counties and used the money to cover the travel, housing, and meal expenses for the group's trip there every second weekend from September to April The course introduced the students to community psychology and to social-intervention theory and practice. The content areas included systems theory; the importance of the historical, social, economic, and political contexts of community problems; critical thinking skills and the analysis of public issues; action-research and community-based consultation; organizational theory and research; an integrative and collaborative approach to comprehensive health planning with providers and consumers indigenous to the area; participatory values and skills, including how to work as a team and with the broader community; learning/experiencing the intractable nature of community problems; and the importance of community capacity-building work to solve community problems. As a group and in teams we spent countless hours over the year defining problems, identifying solutions, mediating differences, evaluating alternatives, selecting best solutions, implementing action strategies, evaluating outcomes, and defining next steps. We spent hundreds of hours processing our work and supporting each other. The course with the nine was the most meaningful and robust pedagogical experience I have ever had as an instructor.

Having commenced with that group of nine in 1971, community-service learning was expanded to 150 undergraduate students in three psychology courses that same year. Some members of the group of nine took leadership roles in creating and supporting the experiences. By the late seventies community-service learning had evolved to include eleven

psychology courses and employed a full-time coordinator and several teaching assistants. In 2006, the program was expanded by Paul Davock, one of
the group of nine, to become a university-wide program: the Centre for
Community Service Learning. In 2008, the centre placed more than 1,600
students from thirty-two courses in 229 community organizations.

Broadly defined, the field of community psychology approaches
human services through a multidisciplinary knowledge base, using an eco-
logical framework and focusing on prevention and health promotion. The
overarching goal is to assist citizens and communities to build their
capacities to improve the overall quality of life by addressing the root
causes of health and social challenges. Community psychologists frequently partner with citizens and their communities as researchers and
consultants to address those challenges. The creation of new settings is
a meaningful form of this capacity-building work.

Over the years, I have been active in the creation of eleven community-based human service settings, four local economic development
ventures, and two academic programs—the free-standing M.A. and Ph.D.
community psychology programs at WLU—and a multidisciplinary
scholarly publication, *The Canadian Journal of Community Mental Health*.
These serve as positive exemplars of community capacity-building work
for the prevention of health and social problems and the promotion of
community well-being. Many of the human service settings and two of
the local economic development ventures were initiated in partnership
with students. Several of the projects provided the material for thesis
projects. The settings demonstrate what can be accomplished through
community–university partnerships.

Created often with community partners, the settings are diverse
and include a developmental centre for children, youth, and adults; a
therapeutic horseback-riding program; a recreation program integrating blind and deaf children with typical children; a community residence for citizens with developmental challenges; a multi-ethnic
housing co-op; a local economic development corporation; a community-shared agriculture project; and a community-based dairy and
cold-storage corporation.

Since 1991, at the request of elders from the Old Order Amish community, I have helped to mediate the clash of values between Old Order
Amish and the dominant social paradigm in agriculture, promoting legal

and socio-political transformation and helping to establish a more equitable balance of power. The transformed public policies have enabled the community to maintain its human and agricultural diversity and small-scale sustainable farm practices.

Community-based economic development (CBED) has complemented the advocacy work. The CBED work included a public education role and the creation of new settings. Outcomes include creating new local capacity in the dairy industry and cold storage of products; assisting numerous farm families to establish sustainable practices such as organic farming; and the successful marketing of farm produce through the creation of the Fair Share Harvest community-shared agriculture (CSA) venture. For over fifteen years locations at WLU (at Regina and Lodge streets) and the Mennonite Central Committee (on Kent Street) served as the late-afternoon weekly drop sites for produce from this "buy fresh, buy local" CSA economic development venture.

It is rare for a person to witness the continuation and growth of their life's work. I am impressed by how far the program in community psychology at WLU has come in the past forty years. The undergraduate offerings and the M.A. and Ph.D. programs rank among the best in North America. I owe a great debt of gratitude to my colleagues who have worked hard to develop a world-class program and to WLU for providing the resources and a welcoming home. Thank you, WLU!

Chapter 12

Our Home on Native Land: Digging Up a Pre-Contact Site (and Beyond)

EDUARD R. RIEGERT

OW DID A MEMBER OF THE WATERLOO LUTHERAN SEMINARY faculty, teaching liturgics (worship) and preaching, become involved in pre-contact archaeology anyway? Well, it was like this.

In the 1960s an expansionist climate permeated the new Waterloo Lutheran University that had replaced Waterloo College at the start of that decade. We were a university now, and new disciplines and developments beckoned. Because the Department of Religious Studies, the Department of Near Eastern Studies, and Waterloo Lutheran Seminary shared many interests, it seemed to make sense to work more closely together in what became the School of Religion and Culture.

In the late 1960s Norman Wagner, the moving force behind this development, opened an intriguing door. Norman, a specialist in Ancient Near Eastern literature and archaeology, called together Lawrence Toombs (an internationally recognized expert in Near Eastern archaeology), Frank Turner (head of the Faculty of Social Work), and me to consider a three-part program focused on Aboriginal people. He envisioned archaeology as the beginning (he and Toombs), followed by study of Aboriginal religion (Riegert), and proceeding to study of the contemporary issues of Aboriginal peoples (Turner). Intriguing—and daunting, for we were to take on these tasks on top of our regular schedules!

A research grant to begin working on a site was obtained from the Lutheran Church in America, the church body with which the seminary was associated at the time, and plans for a systematic excavation of a site went into full swing in 1970. Dean Knight, a graduate student in archaeology at the University of Toronto, helped with selection of what became known as the Moyer Site and with the organization and conduct of the first season's dig. Prominent Canadian archaeologists George MacDonald and Jim Wright encouraged exploration of the site and helped with analysis of artifacts.

Named after the landowners, the Blake Moyers, the site is located some three kilometres northeast of New Dundee, Ontario, about an hour's drive from WLU. A camp was established in a neighbouring orchard, a laboratory was created in a house on Bricker Street, and in May the dig began. While Norman Wagner exercised general supervision of the project, Dean Knight was field director in 1970, Larry Toombs in 1971, and Clarke Mecredy in 1972.

Aboriginal sites in Waterloo County had been recorded in archaeological literature since the late 1800s; the presence of flint and ceramic artifacts at Moyer suggested a possible midden (garbage dump), which would presume a settlement. This supposition was proved correct in 1970 with a series of exploratory trenches that revealed not only a midden but also post moulds (dark stains below the plowed layer of soil) in a continuous line, which proved the existence of a longhouse wall. Excavations in the next two years revealed the extent of the settlement, two more middens, ten longhouses, and parts of a palisade.

It is one thing to find artifacts, post moulds, hearths, middens, and such, and to map each find accurately; it is quite another to analyse, identify, and record each and every artifact and ceramic shard. Artifacts can be measured, photographed, and drawn; pottery analysis is much more intricate because of the wealth of decoration and shapes. The ultimate aim, though, is to be able to compare the artifacts of one site with those of other sites and so, slowly and laboriously, to discover and date whole cultural areas.

Obviously, the analysis, description, and classification of artifacts results in a vast amount of information. Norman was enamored of the new capabilities for recording and analysing data made possible with the computer (a Honeywell had recently been put in place at WLU). Knowing that the full coding of artifacts for storage and analysis by computer had begun in Ontario archaeology, he was eager to develop a code for cataloguing the data from our site. This he and Larry proceeded to

do; an early example of the application of the new technology to archaeology, it is part of the report of the dig, *The Moyer Site: A Pre-Historic Village in Waterloo County* (1974), authored by Norman, Larry, and myself.
(The book was one of the two inaugural publications of the embryonic
Wilfrid Laurier University Press.) For example, the collars of the ceramic
vessels discovered on-site took, in cross-section, at least eight shapes,
while pottery decorations included over 140 patterns. Once such details
are coded for several sites, comparison and analysis by computer are
much more immediate. The site report offers a code and also presents dis-
coveries both photographically and graphically.

By the use of these means, the Moyer site is dated at 1400 C.E., toward
the end of the Middle Ontario Iroquois Stage (1300–1400 C.E.). Because
of its geographical location it is identified as a settlement of the Neutral
nation and part of the Iroquois cultural group. Thus in the Moyer site we
are encountering a people poised on the brink of the historical period
when Europeans like Samuel de Champlain and Jesuit missionaries came
exploring.

Champlain is an invaluable source of information, for he has left
accounts of his journeys from the Ottawa River to the south shore of
Lake Ontario and from Lake Huron to the St. Lawrence River. He encountered nations similar to each other but living in definable areas: the
Hurons north and east of Georgian Bay; the Petuns off the east shore of
Lake Huron; and the Neutrals in a broad band across the north shore of
Lake Erie to the Niagara region. At that point they were close to the Iroquois proper—the confederacy of originally five nations, namely, the
Seneca, Cayuga, Onondaga, Oneida, and Mohawk, strung out along the
south shore of Lake Ontario and curving up along the St. Lawrence. (In
about 1722 these five nations were joined by the Tuscarora nation, who
were pushed out of Carolina by white settlement, to form the present-
day Six Nations Confederacy.)

These nations shared essentially the same culture, since all were not
only hunters and gatherers but also agriculturalists, growing what the
Five Nations called the Three Sisters: corn, beans, and squash. All built
the kind of longhouses we found at Moyer: Quonset-style frameworks
covered with bark, with a series of hearths down the middle, sleeping
bunks along the sides, and storage compartments at the ends for their har-
vests and other food items.

Father Gabriel Lalemant, one of the missionaries based at the mission settlement at Midland, Ontario (Sainte Marie among the Hurons), described the Huron longhouse in winter as a "miniature picture of hell … seeing nothing, ordinarily, but fire and smoke, and on every side naked bodies, black and half roasted, mingled pell-mell with the dogs, which are held as dear as the children of the house…."[1]

Yet it was agriculture that ordered the life of the Neutrals and the other Iroquoian people, and in the planting, growing, harvesting seasons their life was anything but a "picture of hell," with major festivals punctuating the phases of agriculture—including a thanksgiving festival. Champlain, visiting these nations in the early 1600s, called them "a happy people, even though their life is wretched by comparison with ours. They have never known anything better, so they are content with what they have. The staple of their diet is Indian corn mixed with red beans and cooked in a variety of different ways…. They also eat a lot of squash, which they boil or roast over hot coals."[2]

He also described how they made bread out of corn and bean flour, used fish and venison, and even fattened bears for slaughter.

It seems to have been Champlain who gave the Neutrals that name. A few months earlier he had travelled, with a party of Huron warriors, down from Huronia, along the Bay of Quinte, across Lake Ontario to Stoney Point and to Lake Oneida. There they attacked an Iroquois (Five Nations) village, giving them their first encounter with muskets, thus alienating them from the French and moving them to side with the British. He noted that while Hurons and Algonkins carried on raids against the Iroquois, the nation nearest the Iroquois remained neutral, despite having 4,000 warriors. "In fact," he observed, "they are on good terms with both [Hurons and Iroquois] and often eat and drink together like old friends."[3]

In the end, that friendship did not save the Neutrals. White contact altered ancient trading patterns, for the Iroquois lands overlooked trading routes on the St. Lawrence and Hudson rivers. White settlement

---

1   Quoted in Fraser Symington, *The Canadian Indian* (McClelland and Stewart, 1969), p. 102.
2   Samuel D. Champlain, *Voyages to New France 1615–18* (Oberon Press, 1970), pp. 78–80.
3   Ibid., p. 66.

pressed them, and when the beaver population collapsed in their hunting grounds, they reached out for the territories of others. In the 1640s
they fell on the Hurons (recall the burning of Sainte Marie among the
Hurons at present-day Midland, Ontario). By 1649 the Hurons were bro-
ken forever by Iroquois attack, plague, and starvation. "About three hundred found refuge with the French. The remainder—eight or nine
thousand—joined the Ottawas for flight westward or went on their own
to the Ojibway tribes on both sides of upper Lake Huron. They were followed during the next three years by the fragments of their neighbour
tribes, the Petuns and Neutrals."[4]

So, at the Moyer site we were standing with the remains of a people
and a culture enjoying their last century or two before massive changes,
invasion, and violence ended their world.

After Moyer I helped direct the excavation of another Neutral site, near
Ayr. I also participated in some historical archaeology in the excavation
of the Burns pottery near Clinton, Ontario. By that time Dean Knight had
joined the WLU faculty and was pursuing the excavation of a huge Huron
site, thus establishing the archaeological part of Norman Wagner's proposal. It was time to turn to my particular commitment to the project,
namely, the exploration of Native American and Canadian religions. So
in 1976 I took summer courses in that field at the University of Mon-
tana, and then launched two courses in the Religion and Culture department, "The Narrative Expression of Canadian Native Religions" and
"Canadian Native Traditions," which focused on a selected group (e.g.,
Plains Indians). I taught these courses for a dozen or so years, and also
offered the "Narrative Expression" course at WLU's Barrie campus and
was invited to offer it at the University of Waterloo and St. Michael's
College at the University of Toronto.

The "narrativity" angle arose from my growing acquaintance with
Aboriginal myths. I used to read these in the evenings to the students
who shared the archaeological dig camp, and began to ponder how to
interpret these stories. Fortuitously, it was also in these years that an
interest in narrative preaching was growing, and the Lutheran Church in
America was sponsoring a large number of workshops to help its pastors

---

4 Symington, pp. 155–56.

develop a narrative style of preaching, which led me to a steady schedule of workshops, seminars, and lectures in the 1970s and 1980s that took me across Canada and into the northern states and resulted in two books, *Imaginative Shock: Preaching and Metaphor* (1990) and *Hear Then a Story: Plot Possibilities for Story Sermons* (2002).

I do not know if Frank Turner was ever able to begin the third part of the proposal. In light of the young age of the Social Work faculty and the enormity of the task, the proposal was very premature. Nevertheless, I like to think that our efforts awakened a generation of students to the study of First Nations and their culture, including some on the doorstep of the university they were attending.

Part Three

"Lutheran" to "Laurier"

Chapter 13

Putting a New University on the Map

ARTHUR STEPHEN

An interview by Robert Alexander with Arthur Stephen on April 4, 2011.

Arthur Stephen joined Laurier in 1974 as a junior admissions officer. Over the next twenty years he served as director of liaison, as director of institutional relations, and in his last fifteen years as vice-president: advancement responsible for recruitment, public affairs, alumni, and development. He retired in January 2011.

He was president in 1998 of the Canadian Council for the Advancement of Education and received their Outstanding Achievement in Advancement Award in 2003. He was the first Canadian to receive the Steuben Apple Award from the Washington, D.C., Council for Advancement and Support of Education (CASE). In 2004 he was a member of the Commission of Philanthropy for CASE in Washington and a member of the European Union Task Force on Philanthropy in Brussels, 2007.

Q. When and how did you come to WLU?

A. I came to Waterloo Lutheran in 1967. I grew up in Scotland near Perth. I left at 18 and went to England. I was planning on being a cartographer, but my eyesight wasn't good enough for that or for the navy. So I emigrated to Toronto in 1966. I was working in the parks department, cutting grass on the Gardiner Expressway with a guy who was going to Lutheran. I had applied to other universities and didn't even know Lutheran existed. I still have a memory of walking into the Torque Room with the orange

chairs after he dragged me to Waterloo. Out of twenty-some million people in Canada, I had met his roommate earlier in Toronto. He was another
Scot, Ian Richmond, who was doing Purple and Gold plays. I don't know
if I saw that as a sign from above, but that's how I came here.

Q. How did you get hired here?

A. I did a double Honours in History and English over about six years,
some years part-time (driving a truck for Leon's Furniture one year),
graduating in 1973. I went back to Scotland, and six months later history
professor Walter Shelton offered me a scholarship to come back to do an
M.A. I had done my Honours thesis under him.

I came back in the winter, intending to work until I started school
again in the fall. I bumped into a guy in the Torque Room named Ian
Smith who was working in high school recruitment. He said, "I'm leaving for a job with Humber College. I can't get you the job, but it's fun and
I can get you an interview." So I had an interview for assistant admissions
officer with Keith Rae [director of admissions] and Henry Dueck [regis-
trar]. When the admissions officer left two years later in '76, I moved up.

Q. So you were here when WLU became provincial?

A. Yes. Laurier was now trying to make its way as a new university. Frank
Peters was president and Neale Tayler vice-president. We had 2,300 students and a small applicant pool. I went to a CASE conference in Atlanta
and realized that we needed to move from information to recruitment,
which was new territory at that time. I did focus groups to find out what
students really wanted to know. I noticed that the important part was
print brochures, not just the calendar. Working with Barry Lyon I started
to change a lot of the material. By 1978 Laurier had an increase in applications of 8% while all the other fourteen universities had a big decline.
I knew we were changing the face of recruitment. And I started using
film, after talking to Willi Nassau. I hired a friend of his, Fred Gorman,
who had been a cameraman for Patrick Watson [noted producer, director, actor, broadcaster]. Fred taught me cinematography and helped me
complete six Laurier films.

At this point I had actually accepted a position at Guelph. But through
some department chairs' efforts, Peters and Tayler said, "What will it take
to get you to stay?"

"Having my own department."

So they created the Liaison department for me. I was very happy to stay, though I didn't enjoy telling friends at Guelph my decision. I was still working closely with Barry Lyon, integrating film work with print work. When I did a film sequence, the kids would then see the same pictures in the view book. No one else was doing that in those days, even in the US. We were probably unique in packaging everything together based on our focus groups. Actually we were branding without knowing it.

Q. What happened next?

A. I enjoyed working with John Weir. He had great integrity. He was conservative, sometimes a bit too conservative. But he cared a great deal for the institution. He was a powerful academic vice-president under Tayler. When Weir became president, he gave me the whole external relations portfolio, except for fundraising under Marge Miller. I was now supervising both Richard Taylor and Barry Lyon. I found Taylor was underestimated. An old-fashioned guy from *The Record* with an old-fashioned typewriter. Give him five different stories and he would turn them out in twenty-four hours. I wanted him to stay as long as he wanted, but he took early retirement to write novels in Parry Sound.

I was carving out a new department with public affairs and liaison [recruitment] underneath it. Other universities didn't realize it then, but there was a lot of synergy between those areas. Public affairs could do a lot of good for recruitment.

I took a lot of pride in what we did between the watershed year of '78 and the late '80s. In '75 half the student body didn't have 60% in the old Grade 13. Even if they only had 56% they were admitted on probation. We were near the bottom in the pecking order for Ontario scholars, etc. We were taking on Ontario's version of the Ivy League: Toronto, Queen's, Western, McMaster, and Waterloo. By the late '70s we were beginning to capitalize on the introduction of co-op in the business school and, later, internships in the Faculty of Arts and Science. Jim McCutcheon's first-year business classes also increased our prestige as his students would rave about him to prospective students back in high school. In later years, Laura Allen and other profs across the campus had a similar impact. Our athletic reputation also helped attract applicants. Finally, Christine Mather was an outstanding choice as dean to found the Faculty of Music.

As time went on we were designing material just for high school counsellors. We got enough feedback from focus groups to know what was useful for them. Their view of Laurier then improved. Some of the stuff we produced they even told other universities they should be doing. It didn't go down well with my colleagues, but it worked. By the mid-'80s we were putting film and graphics images together. Some of it looks contemporary even now, in spite of being pre-digital. This included narrowing down the branding look of the school from Wilfrid Laurier University to just Laurier and slowly moved that into print. By the end of the '80s we were number three behind Queen's and Waterloo, having passed Western and U. of T.

Q. What followed this period?

A. The next big transition came in '92 when Lorna Marsden was elected president. She was a Canadian senator and associate vice-provost at U. of T. I spent only five years with her, but I learned more from her than anyone else I worked for. I met her in Ottawa when she was president-elect. She said to get ready for her Christmas card list of 1,500 people. She was a politician. She had gravitas as an academic as well as a senator; she had led the status-of-women movement in the '70s.

Now Laurier was getting serious about fundraising. It's important to remember she was president during the Rae years of cutbacks. It was a tough time to raise money. I did some of the PR part of a $6 million campaign in the '80s led by Marge Miller. Marge went on to raise $100 million at Western. She was a terrific fundraiser, maybe the best in Canada. (This was one case of John being too conservative. He should have offered her more to stay; he would have earned it back many times over.) Anyway, Lorna ended up raising $16 million. We would never have reached that figure without her energy.

I had always believed in the synergy of putting the external stuff together. We were the first university in Canada to put recruitment, public affairs, alumni affairs, and development under one umbrella. Nobody else on the continent had added student recruitment to that package. Lorna gave me a full vice-presidency with those four areas. I enjoyed working with her in the '90s. It was no surprise that both UBC and York were interested; she left for York. I tried to convince her to stay, but we lost her.

Another important factor is the architecture, the look and feel of a campus. When you look at the limestone of Western, it gives the campus a special look. Our eclectic brick and stone buildings could use some ivy, so I convinced Lorna to let me do some planting. If the architects screw up, plant vines. What really works for Laurier is the geography. When a kid and his or her parents arrive at Alumni Hall and with a guide do the circle tour of the Peters Building, the Torque Room, and down into the Athletic Complex and then back by the residences, the campus is not overwhelming. They can get anywhere in a few minutes. That is such a simple idea, but it's one of the major factors in Laurier's success. The Torque Room as the central hub even today allows some 12,000 students to feel they are part of a small community. Perception is reality. The administration makes a mistake if they try to brand Laurier as medium-sized.

Q. And then?

A. I worked with President Bob Rosehart for the next 10 years. He was the total opposite of Lorna. He was an engineer, and it was lucky for us that he was around when buildings were needed for the double cohort. Bob was a good guy to work for. He was the centre of the community at Thunder Bay when he left Lakehead. Bob was very good at adopting the Laurier persona in a way that was fun to watch, with the alumni and others. He was especially good at local politics.

Q. Any other challenges?

A. Yes. I played a role along with Terry Copp in the founding of the Brantford campus. It began with a call from Terry to meet with the young mayor, Chris Friel, who had a real vision for the city. The idea of having a satellite campus came up and I took it back to Bob. He became passionate about it, went down to work with the mayor and city council. We thought it was going to be a local campus helping the farm kids who couldn't afford to get to Hamilton or Waterloo. We underestimated the power of the 403 highway. If we had been told in 1999 that the campus would grow to 2,300 students, the size of WLU back in the '60s, we'd have said you were dreaming. The business school, along with the Faculty of Music, helped the reputation of Laurier big-time.

The other thing that happened in the '90s was the new phenomenon of magazine rankings. In the issue of *Maclean's* that began ranking universities, we were forty-second out of forty-five, in spite of making the long climb up the quality ladder. I spent a year working with and lobbying *Maclean's* to show them that they were using the US private/public system, which put 35% value on the financial. By the second year, they revised the categories to fit the Canadian context, dropping the financial index to 10%. Our ranking was now in the top three of our category. Without this change, the work of our last fifteen years would have disappeared. That is as close as I came to having a nervous breakdown. The changes I lobbied for were even-handed, so that they had some chance of being accepted. It also helped that our chancellor at the time, Willard Estey, was on *Maclean's* board. Having spent so much time on rankings, I began giving seminars in Australia and the UK on how to deal with rankings.

Q. Anything else?

A. I had so many talented people to work with over 35 years. Helene Amster played a major role in changing Laurier recruiting. Lynne Hanna, who worked with me in the '80s and '90s in institutional relations, was incredibly talented. Valerie Clark Withiam, Drew Ness, and Jennifer Casey were seminal figures in developing our province-leading recruitment program. Debbie Lou Ludolph played a major role in recruitment and public affairs in the '80s and '90s. In this century Glennice Snyder has carried on the tradition of leading recruitment to new records in attracting high school students to Laurier.

We made a habit of hiring our co-op students to do our travelling. They were embodiments of what the kids wanted to be. So when they talked to high school kids, they would wait until the end of the session before saying, "By the way, we're students and are going back to Laurier in the fall."

And Charles Kennedy and Brian Breckles launched major alumni initiatives in the '90s and the 2000s that still bear fruit.

Q. Do you remember incidents that did not work so well?

A. Absolutely. We published a brochure about internships. One was about a student at some nineteenth-century historical place. The picture showed a guy hacking a chicken to death in full colour. Even though the chicken was rubber, I was not quick enough to be aware of how offensive it would be.

There was also the panty raid fiasco in 1989. It may not have been the worst thing that could have happened, but it was shortly after the Polytechnique Montreal murder of fourteen women students. Also, you know you're in trouble when the satellite TV trucks get here and you are setting up a commission to report back in six weeks!

Another time, Lynne Hanna and I were doing a major tabloid report to the community, printing it at the *Beacon Herald* in Stratford. I went to Stratford and brought a copy back to her place to look at. A few minutes later, we saw that the headline spelled "community" with three m's. We couldn't get to them by phone so we had to get a cabbie in Stratford to go over and say the famous line, "Stop the presses!" Luckily, they were stopped at 14,000; the print run had been 120,000.

Q. How have you ended your career?

A. I spent the last two years of my term on a sabbatical that ended January 1, 2011. I had been editing my photos over the last few years and will continue to do so. I will keep active as a board member of the Laurier Centre for Military Strategic and Disarmament Studies. Fred Nichols didn't want to retire. He's still in touch with alumni and donors fifteen years later. He has raised more money than anyone else since he came in the '60s.

Q. What are your plans for the next few years?

A. I will remain active. Apart from coaching varsity squash for a decade or so, I always enjoyed working with athletics. I gathered a lot of photography from Jim Hertel and myself. I chaired Laurier's seventy-fifth anniversary (1986) and am now working on Laurier's 100th-year athletic history.

Chapter 14

The Perks and Perils of a
University Photographer

JAMES HERTEL

J BEGAN MY CAREER AT WLU ON SEPTEMBER 1, 1977. I WAS
overjoyed to finally have a job as a professional photographer. I was
hired by Willi Nassau and Dr. Flora Roy. My title was University Photographer and I maintained that title until retirement two years ago in 2009.

In the early days they were so worried that I would not have enough
work to keep me busy that Willi and Dr. Norm Wagner made a joint
purchase of a graphic-arts camera and processor so I could do photography of final artwork and galleys for WLU Press and the print shop.
I had a background in this work from five years at the University of
Waterloo and three years in the printing industry. It was while working at the University of Waterloo that I met and became good friends
with Murray Corman, who came to Laurier and took command of the
print shop.

Laurier was a fun as well as a demanding place to work. Many events
and tight deadlines meant long hours shooting and processing film.
Working weekends happened frequently. I photographed "everyone":
students, staff, faculty, top executives, administrators, and high-profile
politicians. And buildings and events.

One Monday I came into work and to my surprise my cupboard of
equipment was empty. I thought we had been robbed. I went to Willi in
a panic. He laughed and said he had sent all of my equipment to the
archaeology dig at Tell el-Hesi in Israel that Larry Toombs and WLU students were working on. Willi and I made a trip to Joe's Camera and

bought all new equipment, the one and only time I went through a camera store with a shopping cart and filled it.

We were working on the seventy-fifth-anniversary book. It was decided that we needed a nighttime shot of the university and surrounding area. Arrangements were made for me to go up on the roof of the Marsland Centre to take the photos. It was winter and a clear, bitterly cold evening. The elevator went just shy of the roof. I took my gear to an outside access where there was a ladder attached to the building that you had to climb to get to the roof. I had a bag with three cameras, two tripods, and extra batteries, film, and lenses. I took the equipment up in two trips. The roof was flat and covered with snow with no railing to stop one from falling. I looked for the best locales. I did the city of Waterloo first, shooting with a Hasselblad and a Canon, bracketing as much as possible and overexposing to be sure of getting what was needed. My batteries in both cameras died from the cold. My hands were shaking while I was trying to change the batteries, so I took off my gloves to gain control. A gust of wind came up and blew my glove to the edge of the rooftop. I very carefully and nervously crawled to the edge and grabbed the glove just as another gust of wind came up that surely would have blown it over the ledge. I secured the tripods, put the cameras in the equipment bag, and headed down the ladder to a safer and warmer place to change batteries and film and calm myself down. I went back up to the roof and finished the assignment. I packed up all my gear and went home · tired, cold, and relieved that that perilous assignment was over.

I have always been afraid of heights. But I had to take aerial photos of the university. I had never been up in an airplane before. Bas Healey from the School of Business and Economics was the pilot, and people from geography went up as well. We had to get shots for students to use for stereo mapping. While we were in the air Bas looked at my hands, which were turning white as I was trying not to show fear, only to be failing badly at it. I had said no to taking the door off before we went up, so Bas had to tilt the aircraft quite a bit so we could get the shots. While I was taking pictures I noticed that a red light was flashing on the dash and a buzzer would sound. I asked if something was wrong and was told that all was well. I kept on taking photos. We came back to the airport with turbulence that caused our light aircraft to land a bit awkwardly but safely. When we landed Bas told me that he was flying slow so I could

get the best pictures, and the buzzing sound was the engine's way of
warning it might stall.

Up in the air again! This time I was with Cam McIntosh from Pirak
Studio, which had been contracted to take photos for the university. We
were to take photos of the university using digital and film. The door of
the plane had been removed, and Cam was seated in the front seat next
to that open space. He was well belted in. I was in the back seat beside a
window with cameras in a bag. I was shooting Hasselblad and digital. We
flew low over downtown Waterloo and Kitchener so Cam could get some
special shots. We encountered some ugly downdrafts. My camera bag
loaded with gear lifted off the seat. I lunged for it, terrified a camera or
lens could slip out and fall, causing serious damage. But we got our shots,
and I was thankful to set foot on the ground again with equipment (and
photographers) intact.

Convocations were very busy times. I used to set up well ahead of
time in a press box at the Waterloo Recreation Centre so I could photograph the recipients of honorary degrees as they were being hooded.
There was a tripod and camera with telephoto lens and a pre-focus on
where that would happen. Then I would go down on the floor and take
candid shots of students, staff, and faculty, and anxious proud parents trying to get shots of their graduating sons and daughters. I wore a black
graduation gown so parents would realize I was working and shouldn't
interrupt me. As the faculty were being led in, I would head for the press
box, climb the stairs to the top, and get ready to start shooting. I would
photograph the honorary-degree recipient until he or she would start
speaking. Then, as quickly as possible, I would pack up all the many pieces
of my equipment and run with this heavy burden down the steps to the
floor to take photos of the recipients as they were speaking—hoping that
along the way no one would suddenly step into my path and cause a very
embarrassing moment in front of some 4,000 people. As time went on,
multiple honorary degrees were awarded and I did more frequent running up and down the dreaded stairs to the press box. Despite the perils,
the perks included working with and photographing some of the most
interesting high-profile people around and being there with the students
on their special day, their teachers, and their proud parents.

I enjoyed my time at Laurier. I watched it grow from a small closely
knit university to what it is today, a significant presence in post-second-

ary education in Canada. Seeing photos I took over the years displayed around the university and appearing in publications is very gratifying. Over the years I won two Photographer of the Year awards. One was from the Council for Advanced Study and Education and the other from the University Photographers Association of America. I am the only Canadian to have won both of these awards.

Chapter 15

A University Press Comes into Being

DOREEN ARMBRUSTER

ILFRID LAURIER UNIVERSITY PRESS OWES ITS EXISTENCE TO Norman E. Wagner, whose vision set in motion the events that led to the establishing of the Press in 1974 and who served as its first director.[1]

In 1973 I was a stay-at-home mom who was quite contented to earn some pocket money by typing term papers, theses, and dissertations for faculty members and students at Waterloo Lutheran University and the University of Waterloo. This allowed me to spend July and August camping with our three children close to the beach at Port Elgin on Lake Huron. Life was great!

Then one day I got a phone call from Norman, whose Ph.D. dissertation I had typed a few years earlier, telling me that he was serving as executive director of the Council on the Study of Religion (CSR) along with his duties as dean of Graduate Studies at WLU. He and some of his colleagues in the CSR were dismayed by the length of time it took to get their books and articles published and were hoping to get their research into print sooner either by taking on the task themselves of preparing camera-ready copy for publication by the CSR or by a newly forming

---

1 It must be noted that this article deals only with the production area of Wilfrid Laurier University Press. Other areas—e.g., accounting, order filling, etc.—were no less important for the functioning of the Press but have not been mentioned as my tenure was spent entirely in production.

press run by and for scholars. The CSR and the Press shared production facilities, under a symbiotic relationship between the two that Norman had worked out with the university.

At the time Bonnie Quinn was the sole person Norm had employed to carry out his vision, and he told me he needed a "fast and accurate typist" to input copy on an IBM Magnetic Tape Selectric Composer, which recorded the keystrokes on a tape. This tape was then loaded into an IBM Electronic Selectric Composer which printed out the text but required someone to manually change the Selectric ball wherever the text called for a font change. The operator also had to instruct the composer about where to divide words at the end of lines—both of these obviously very slow and tedious operations. The text thus produced was then manually pasted up into the final page format.

Norm felt that I would be the right person to serve as that typist and was not willing to take no for an answer. When I told him that my youngest child would only be starting kindergarten in September and that I would not leave her with a babysitter, he responded that I would only need to work the hours that she was at school. When I told him that I wanted to be able to spend the summer at the beach with the children, he said I could take July and August off. Seeing that he had countered all of my objections, I agreed to begin working in September of 1973. Fast forward: in less than two years I was working full-time and was making arrangements for childcare for the summer months.

It was not long before Norm realized that more hours of inputting were required to meet the printing deadlines, and so it was decided that I would contact Reta Lienhardt, a friend of mine who was also doing typing for faculty members and students at home, to try to convince her to work part-time inputting text. Thus began a career of fifteen years at the Press for Reta. Early in 1974, production in the areas of printing out the camera-ready text and in pasting up the final pages was getting bogged down and it was time to hire an additional staff member. That turned out to be Heather McCullough.

In May 1974 our Publications Office was officially incorporated as Wilfrid Laurier University Press. Within a few years I was promoted to the position of Production Coordinator, a position I held until my retirement in 1998, when I was succeeded by Heather (now Heather Blain-Yanke). My part-time hours and summer lay-offs were now a thing of the past.

It was also in 1974 that Harold Remus came to Waterloo as Norman's assistant in the Executive Office of the CSR, with duties at the Press thrown in alongside his teaching. Harold was a very experienced and capable editor and I worked very closely with him on many publications for both the Press and the CSR. I owe a tremendous debt to Harold for all that he taught me in those years. When Norman left WLU in 1978 to become the president of the University of Calgary, Harold succeeded him both as executive officer of the CSR and as director of WLU Press. My close association with Harold continued until he retired as director in 1983. Harold's successor as director was Sandra Woolfrey, who held the position from 1983 until 1999. Sandra was in turn succeeded by Brian Henderson, who is still the director. With their varying personal styles of leadership, each of these directors steered the Press through the various stages of its development.

Much of my story has to do with the technologies of getting words into type and thence into books and journals. Around 1975, for example, it became apparent that a more efficient typesetting system was needed. Harold Remus and I travelled to Toronto to visit a company that was using a Mergentaler V-I-P (Variable Input Phototypesetter) to produce galleys of camera-ready copy which were then pasted by hand into camera-ready pages. Again using a special IBM Selectric ball in an IBM typewriter, I typed the text onto special sheets of paper. These were then sent to the Toronto company, where they were scanned to produce "tickertape" that was fed into their phototypesetter to produce camera-ready galleys. These were then mailed to Waterloo, where our staff pasted them up into pages.

This system proved to have so many pitfalls that within a year or so we decided to purchase two paper-tape perforators so that we could input the text directly to produce the yards and yards of tickertape needed to produce the galleys for a journal article or a book chapter. By this time a representative from a company in London, which also used a Mergenthaler V-I-P, was picking up our large rolls of paper tape and a few days later delivering the galleys for paste-up. After a year or so of using this service we found a company in Kitchener named Dumont Graphics, located in the space now occupied by St. John's Kitchen at Victoria and Weber streets. Dumont used the same V-I-P machine, which meant we could deliver our tapes there and pick up the camera-ready galleys, often on the same day. Some years later, in 1984, the Press hired Steve Izma, a former employee of Dumont. Steve is still on staff at WLUP, in the capacity of Computing Systems Administrator.

In 1977 we had the opportunity to purchase a used Mergenthaler V-I-P of our own. While this was a rather daunting proposition, as it meant learning how to run and troubleshoot problems with this monster, it also allowed us to be more efficient in our production process. The Mergenthaler company had a training centre in Pennsylvania, and Carl Langford of Computing Services at WLU and I spent a week there learning to become comfortable with this machine and also with the accompanying developer (and the chemicals it required) for the photographic film used to produce the output.

At the time the Press was located in what had been the dining room and bedrooms of what had served for a while as the president's house. Rechristened Centre Hall and then later Alumni Hall, it housed Graduate Studies below ground level, with the attached garage divided between Victor Martens' voice studio and our stock of publications. Adjoining our production area on the main floor was the large room used for university functions. The V-I-P was a formidable presence. It measured about six feet long, four feet wide, and five feet high and made loud honking noises (much like a gaggle of geese flying overhead) as the drum spun around to locate characters on the photographic film fonts mounted on the drum. It was not unusual to have guests in the reception area wander into our area to investigate the source of those strange honkings.

By 1978 our production staff included three people inputting text on the paper-tape perforators and running out galleys on the V-I-P and three people pasting up the pages in another room. We were quite proud of our production system and felt that our staff had worked very hard (often ingeniously) to overcome the challenges facing us. Norman arranged with the local television station to report on our operation. Huddled around a TV set for the six-o'clock news, we saw our operation displayed and an interview with Norman—who to our surprise stated that "our production system was so simple that 'anyone off the street' could be trained to do it." We never let Norman forget those immortal words.

To say that our facilities in Centre/Alumni Hall were overcrowded would be a gross understatement. There was barely enough space in the production room to walk between the desks and machines. At times we oozed over into the kitchen and the big reception room to do specific tasks or to hold staff meetings. Add to that the noise generated by the V-I-P and the heat emitted by the developer and computers—hardly ideal conditions for either the hard-working staff or labouring machine. What wonderful news it was, then, to learn in 1991 that we were being granted space in the building being renovated at 202 Regina Street. We would have a separate soundproof room for the V-I-P, plus a darkroom for loading the phototypesetting paper, and a sink to do our weekly wash-up of the developer components. I would have a computer desk in the production area plus a separate office to meet with authors, editors, and others in a quiet atmosphere. It would be like heaven after the crowded space of Alumni Hall. The highlight of our move was to see the crane that lifted the V-I-P from the outside deck of Alumni Hall onto the truck that would transport it to its new location.

The next progression in the production process was to phase out the paper-tape perforators and replace them with computers interfaced with the Mergenthaler V-I-P. Thanks are due to Hart Bezner of Computing Services for making this a possibility. Hart and Norman were long-time friends and had developed many solutions to various problems and needs at the Press over the years, which meant Hart was quite familiar with the Press's progress and always stepped in as needed.

Eventually the V-I-P was retired to Mergenthaler heaven, replaced by a laser printer. By this time we were using a computerized typesetting system that incorporated final page makeup. This meant that manual page makeup was now redundant; it remains only as a memory in the history of the Press.

I have lost count of the number of new typesetting systems I learned during my twenty-five years at the Press, but I do recall thinking each time I was faced with learning a new one that it would surely be the last—but then there was always another new one to master. Of course, once we had the new system under our belts we were always pleasantly surprised at our new efficiencies.

Today much of the actual production is outsourced and so the production staff is fewer in number than in my time. Judging by the number of new titles on the Press's backlist, this is obviously not a negative factor.

During my years at the Press, I enjoyed many long-term working relationships with the managing editors of the journals we produced and with some of our authors. John McMenemy heads the list, since he served as managing editor of the *Canadian Journal of Political Science/Revue canadienne de science politique* for approximately three decades; I worked closely with him for about twenty-three of those years. For a number of years John arranged to bring the editorial board of the journal to Waterloo, where we demonstrated the many stages of getting the journal into print in hopes of eliminating some common problems and also acquainting them with WLU in the process. During my tenure, Peter Richardson of the University of Toronto, Willi Braun of the University of Alberta, and Harold Remus, Peter Erb, and Kay Koppedrayer of WLU all served terms as managing editors of *Studies in Religion/Sciences Religieuses,* the omnibus journal in religious studies in Canada produced by the Press from the mid-1970s until very recently. Many others could be mentioned, but it would exceed space limitations. To all of them I owe a debt of gratitude for the many things I learned during my association with them and for many good memories from those times. Very special among them are the times when Edna Staebler invited our entire staff to her cottage home on Sunfish Lake, where we shared a meal and listened to the many fascinating stories she recounted of her life and work.

My twenty-five years at Wilfrid Laurier University Press passed by very quickly and I'm very thankful to Norman Wagner for giving me the opportunity to have such an interesting career. In retirement, I've continued my association with the Press: working from home, I'm currently producing the second-last of the sixteen volumes of the Press's landmark edition of the writings of Florence Nightingale, edited by Lynn McDonald. Then it will be more time on the golf links, here in Ontario and in Florida during the winter months.

Chapter 16

Procurement: A New Day

BOB REICHARD

O N FEBRUARY 1976 A NEW DEPARTMENT CAME INTO BEING AT Wilfrid Laurier University. In an upstairs back bedroom of a house on Bricker Street, over offices of the Physical Plant and Planning Department, a new purchasing department became a reality.

I was in the purchasing department at the University of Waterloo at the time, but an ad for a buyer at WLU caught my eye. I applied and got the job, reporting to Cliff Bilyea, Business and Personnel Manager. His secretary, Elizabeth Miller, who also did the typing for the whole department, was terrific in helping me to become oriented to the university environment. I soon discovered that, like the times, things at this "new" university were a-changin'. And through the new department where I was now situated I became very involved in many of those changes.

After arranging for office furniture, a telephone, and dictating and copying equipment, I settled in to establish a presence on campus through meetings with individuals and departments, to determine their needs and provide purchasing advice and assistance when required.

Purchasing policies and procedures needed attention, and I set to work on some new ones. It was a very complex process—interviewing and consulting with WLU departments, purchasing departments at other universities, and government agencies. The result was a "Purchasing Bible," as it were. Many meetings with WLU departments followed to acquaint them with the new procedures and to clarify any concerns about them. Many departments were glad to relinquish the buying chore and

86

concentrate on their prime purposes, whether teaching and research or service functions. Others, however, saw it as an intrusion into an area where they had been totally in charge. Over time, most were won over and saw the benefits of a centralized procurement system.

Another "new" was to do something about the hodge-podge of campus furnishings. In consultation with departments and furniture manufacturers, a standard for office furniture and equipment was established that over time did away with the hodgepodge and also realized cost savings by purchasing in volume.

Technology was ever changing, and when managing the telephone system was added to our department's responsibility it shortly became apparent that the old "cord and plug" system had to be upgraded to digital. The contract was awarded to Musitron Communications. It was a major project, as new cable had to be installed to accommodate the new equipment without disturbing the day-to-day operations of the university.

A new purchasing strategy called system contracting was introduced for purchase of plumbing, electrical, janitorial, and stationery supplies. It allowed university departments to order directly from designated suppliers.

As the workload grew, new staff were required. Lilly Amos was added as departmental secretary, relieving Elizabeth Miller of that responsibility. Other new staff in that position over the years were Laurie Royce, Marylou Shagena, Brenda Donelle, and Anita Moore. Further departmental growth required the addition of a buyer, Karin Tamm, and then, later, Jennifer Kohli as assistant buyer. After some years, Karin moved on to FedEx and Marion Barnaby was hired as her replacement. Marion's start at the university was not without surprise, as a few weeks after her hiring she announced something quite new: she was expecting, which I believe was as much a shock to her and her husband, Wayne, as it was to me. However, not long after the new arrival, she was back at work.

Still another new question landed in our department: How to keep track of all the capital equipment in the many departments at this ever-growing university? John Banikoff was hired on a one-year contract to implement a capital-equipment inventory-control system to identify, record, and keep track of all that equipment. This was right up John's alley, as this had been his occupation before he retired. The process, which took slightly more than a year, greatly simplified the tracking of the equipment.

Two characters—a term I use advisedly—with whom I had daily contact were Joe Wey of Janitorial Services and Grounds and Gerry Donelle in Shipping and Receiving. Joe looked after all of the moving on campus and was of great assistance to our department in getting furniture and other goods to the right place at the right time. Gerry was responsible for getting all the goods received by the university to the departments quickly while processing all of the paperwork required by our department, the requisitioning departments, and the accounts-receivable section of the Business Office.

Gerry was also the campus' practical joker. But, to the delight of his victims, he was caught out in the "Billy Crystal Affair" concocted by Murray Corman, John Durst, and me, along with others. Gerry had heard a Billy Crystal tape while he, his wife Joan, and the Cormans were at our place for dinner one Saturday. He said he would like to have a copy, so Murray and I cooked up a scheme to place a dummy order to Sam the Record Man in Toronto for a dozen tapes. Gerry got the receiving copy and phoned to say he wanted the order cancelled. We pretended to grant his wish but got twelve used tapes from John Durst in Audio-Visual, wrapped them in brown paper with a dummy label from Sam's, put some postage on the parcel in the mailroom, kicked it around a bit to make it look like it had come through the mail, and put it in Gerry's mailbox. When Gerry picked up his mail he was furious. When he stormed into my office with the parcel, I ripped off the wrapping paper and asked him to deliver the tapes to John Durst. He was absolutely nonplussed. He said we would pay for our prank, and that still may happen—but it was worth it.

Another "new": after the sudden and unexpected passing of Murray, who had been the manager of Printing and Mail Services, those responsibilities were also added to Purchasing, and we became the Materiel Management Department. We were then responsible for purchasing, shipping and receiving, surplus disposal, capital inventory control, printing, mail services, furniture inventory, and telephone services.

And, once again, a telephone system was required to replace the existing one, which had become overloaded and obsolete. The installation, by Bell Canada, was not without its problems, but they were resolved and the new system went into operation, much to everyone's satisfaction. The new system had all the call features available at that time and was a great assistance to the administrative staff. Shortly after the new system was installed, it was determined that it really belonged more in the realm of Computing Services and was transferred to them.

Finally, July 1996: I took my leave of Wilfrid Laurier University to assume what I thought was a well-deserved retirement. Marion Barnaby assumed the helm in my place.

My time at Wilfrid Laurier was a very happy and rewarding part of my life and I enjoyed every minute of it. The many friends that I made while there have remained good friends, and I cherish them all.

Chapter 17

The Library—Growing with
a Growing University

JOHN ARNDT

A S AN ALUMNUS OF WATERLOO LUTHERAN UNIVERSITY (1964), IT was something of a homecoming to join the library in 1967 after earning my B.L.S. from the University of Toronto. As a student, and later as a librarian, I was privileged to be part of the library's expansion, serving as head of information services, of collections management, and finally of acquisitions until my retirement in 1998.

There are four periods in the development of the library. Each period includes the holdings and acquisitions of the seminary as well as those of the college and the university. The first and longest period is that of 1911 to 1959—the barest beginnings on into the Waterloo College era. The second is the era of Waterloo Lutheran University, from 1960 to 1973—a period of moderate growth and space challenges. The third, 1973 to the 1990s, was a period of increased funding, growth, and development of automated services. The fourth, the 1990s to the present, was a time of library cooperation, joint electronic services, and collection building.

When the Waterloo College Associate Faculties became the new University of Waterloo in 1959, change came to Waterloo College and its library. Librarian Doris Lewis departed for the University of Waterloo leaving behind a library staff and a collection that were both small. The Rev. Erich Schultz, a young librarian with a theological education, was hired as the chief librarian of Waterloo Lutheran University and Waterloo Lutheran Seminary. Erich related many times that he was told by the president of the time to be diligent in not allowing any of the collection to be transferred to the new school down the street.

There were nine staff members in the library at that point, two of whom remained with the library to retirement: Margaret Wettlaufer and Norma McClenaghan, both still active in WLU affairs. There was no formal relationship between the two libraries until 1970, when a cooperative lending policy allowed direct borrowing between the University of Waterloo and Waterloo Lutheran University libraries for faculty, graduate students, and cross-registered students, and soon thereafter for undergraduate students.

Following in the footsteps of former library instructors, Mabel Dunham (the long-serving librarian of the Kitchener Public Library) and Doris Lewis, the new chief librarian, offered a compulsory (pass/fail) library instruction course, which was a requirement for graduation. Erich learned, years later, that the registrar allowed some students (including me) who had transferred from other universities to be exempted from taking the course. It was difficult for Erich to believe that anyone could have slipped through his net.

A major undertaking early on was the conversion of the collection from the Dewey Decimal classification to the Library of Congress classification, which, when completed in the early 1960s, put the library's classification system in harmony with that of most North American academic libraries.

The library had been in Willison Hall since 1914, and by 1961 the collection of about 23,000 items occupied two floors, with books in the old gymnasium on the bottom floor, and reserve, government publications, interlibrary loans, and serials on the main floor. Because of the meagre collection, young history students had to be creative in following the policies of professors such as Loren Calder and Welf Heick, who insisted on the use of primary sources. Of course, there was interlibrary loan, but, unfortunately, it took six to eight weeks for the material to arrive, if it came at all.

It was soon evident that Willison Hall was inadequate for an expanding library collection and a rapidly growing student body. In 1960 there were 640 full time students, but by 1965 the students numbered more than 2,146. A new library building officially opened in September 1965 with initial plans of three floors to house 150,000 volumes to serve 600 students. However, financial restraints limited construction to two floors with the main and second floors sitting on what appeared to be stilts. Finally, sensitive to the growing need for student space on campus and in the library, the Board of Governors gave permission to enclose the lower floor of the library to create additional classrooms and to provide space for library receiving and storage. This was the beginning of the university's "tradition" of providing much-needed space for the library but requiring it to share the space with classrooms and campus departments.

Starting in 1965, staffing increased with the hiring of three professional librarians: for reference, cataloguing, and government documents. The total number of staff was thus twenty, plus a number of students employed to work at the circulation desk and to provide evening service.

The reference librarian was responsible for interlibrary loan, a service limited to faculty and graduate students and completely dependent on the vagaries of the post office. After finding the location of the book or journal through bibliographical publications such as the National Union Catalogue, the reference librarian placed the request form in an envelope along with the appropriate postage for return mail. Occasionally, mistakes were made, one of the most common being the enclosure of Canadian stamps for requests going to the United States. In 1970 Marcella Roth (now Marcella Martin) was hired to work in interlibrary loans, thus freeing up the librarian for reference work. Marcella's use of the newly introduced teletyping machine and many other technological innovations over the years made service much more efficient. She remained as interlibrary loan manager until her retirement and is remembered by students and faculty for her conscientious service.

Provincialization of the university in 1973 brought an increase in funding for staffing and collections. Within a year the library had added twelve new staff, bringing the total to fifty-two. The library became more involved in provincial cooperative projects, one being the Inter-University Transit Service, which connected all Ontario universities, the National Library, and the National Science Library. It also meant that the library was able to take advantage of new technologies. As many will still recall, the principal library technologies of the time were the card catalogues, electric typewriters, microfilm readers, music-listening equipment, teletyping machine, and a photocopier for on-demand copying by students, faculty, and staff. When the university installed its mainframe computer, a systems expert, Herb Schwartz, was hired to develop library computer services. Automated services were introduced into the library after extensive consultation with staff and thorough testing of prototype systems. Acquisitions was the first department to be automated, followed by cataloguing and cataloguing processing, government documents, and circulation. The public online catalogue, QCAT, was the final development.

The library automation project was created completely in-house using the MSQ database management system software developed at WLU. It was the largest of ninety MSQ systems being used on campus with many more capabilities than most commercial systems and enabled the library to be, as Erich Schultz proclaimed, "masters of our own fate."

With the introduction of the public online catalogue, the card catalogue was closed. Even though no records were being added to it, a few users, including some faculty, tended to favour the familiar card catalogue. At the end of 1991, the cabinets were removed and thousands of cards recycled, freeing up space for more terminals and CD-ROM workstations.

Erich Schultz had retired by the time most of the automation was in place. It was the responsibility of the next chief librarian, Virginia Gillham, to advance the library to another stage of computerization. To take advantage of the opportunities offered by new technologies and delivery systems, the libraries of Wilfrid Laurier, the University of Guelph, and the University of Waterloo entered into a formal agreement of cooperation with the formation of the Tri-University Group (TUG). Joint task groups representing key areas of the library—acquisitions and serials, cataloguing, circulation and reserve, public access, and systems operations—worked together in the selection of one library system from the many available that most closely satisfied the needs of the three libraries. The TUG libraries also established policies for collection and serials rationalization, joint storage, interlibrary loan and document delivery, joint projects for electronic journals, and a single automated catalogue system.

By the end of the 1990s, a seamless integration of library collections and services with one information resource was in place for users at the three institutions. Three catalogue databases were merged into one but appeared as a single bibliographic record representing the holdings of the three libraries. A catalogue search could be carried out in the library as well as electronically from one's on-campus office or from home. Online databases provided access to electronic journals and indexing and abstracting services, many with full text information.

While the library had a state-of-the-art computer system, the offices and holdings were housed in a building designed in 1965. On the basis of recommendations by library consultant Margaret Beckman, a Waterloo College graduate and long-time chief librarian at the University of Guelph, a renovation project was initiated in 2002 to modernize the library. Carrying it out disrupted library service for almost a year, with staff relocated to the St. Michael's campus, the collection housed in trailers on the Seagram lot, and reference service provided in a tent near the Central Teaching Building. The circulation desk was situated on the landing outside the main doors of the library with power provided by a long electrical cord stretching from the main building. Although it was possible to obtain a few WLU publications, most students and faculty used the University of Waterloo library.

Fortunately, the weather was mild in that fall of 2002. Although the building inspector would not allow public access to the library, staff, including the new chief librarian, Sharon Brown, worked in the basement until the renovations were completed in January 2003. This was only one of a number of challenges affecting the library and the university, others being the support-staff strike in 2002 and the most recent library renovation project in 2005.

Over the years, the library has benefited from the goodwill of individuals in providing gifts-in-kind as well as much-needed funding for collections and other services. Recently the generosity of alumni, students, and parents of students have enabled the library to provide services that it could not otherwise afford. Alumni provided $200,000 in assistance toward the 2005 renovations, while undergraduate students will be providing $500,000 over eight years through the Student Life Levy for laptop computers and back issues of electronic journals. The Graduate Student Association is providing funding for research materials and a graduate study area of more than a thousand square feet, which includes a lounge. Corporate donors are important. Recently, Sun Life Financial donated $75,000 for the library's Digital Studio in honour of the retirement of Robert Astley. An anonymous donor funded the GEO Special Data Centre. These gifts are an indication that the library is, as it always has been, a quintessential part of the university.

With years come memories. The wonderful Christmas parties with gift exchanges, mad skits, and informal fun. Another is Erich's fastidiousness concerning the no-food-or-drink policy in the library. From his office window he could see everyone entering the library. If he spotted anyone—student, staff, or faculty—carrying a cup of coffee into the library, he would dash out of his office and confront the offender. For me there are many fond memories connected with working in a place I loved on the campus of the institution—or its early embodiment—from which I had graduated.

Chapter 18

The Computer Comes to WLU: Honeywell 316, Xerox Sigma 7— and Great People

HART BEZNER

O N THE 1960S ELECTRONIC COMPUTING BECAME AN IMPORTANT component on many university campuses, especially at research-intensive institutions. The development and standardization of the simple computer language FORTRAN—the name a contraction of FORmula TRANslation—made it relatively easy to program the machines. FORTRAN was particularly suited for scientific work. For business applications COBOL (COmmon Business Oriented Language) was developed.

Personal, interactive computing was still a dream and a hope. Programs and data were punched on cards and fed to the machines by special operators who printed the results and handed the cards and output back to the users. This arrangement was known as "batch processing."

Users would develop their programs in FORTRAN, COBOL, or other specialized languages, punch them onto cards, often hundreds of them, number them sequentially to protect against a spill, and submit these to the operator. After a few hours, or after a few days, the cards would be processed and the resulting output returned. The error messages would be deciphered and the programs patched and resubmitted. For complicated programs it would often take weeks to get things working properly.

When I came to WLU in 1967 the university had no in-house hardware, but computing was encroaching. The Registrar's Office, for example, punched student data on cards and had these taken to IBM for processing. And then there was Jim Kitchen in the School of Business, a visionary at the time, who saw great potential in personal, interactive computing. He would arrange for on-campus demonstrations of the emerging interactive BASIC language developed at Dartmouth College.

There was also Duncan MacLulich of the Biology department. IBM had developed an interesting remote-access station called QUIKTRAN. It consisted of a card reader and a printer and a telephone link to an IBM computer in Toronto. Programs, written in FORTRAN, could be submitted and the output received within minutes. A QUIKTRAN station had been installed in Willison Hall, and Duncan was one of the early academic users of the system.

The Physics department soon began to incorporate a computing component. A teletype unit was installed in the Arts Building, students punched FORTRAN programs onto the teletype's yellow paper tape, dialed a computer in Ann Arbor, Michigan, ran the paper tape through the teletype, and within seconds the output was printed.

The Ann Arbor computer was operated by a time-sharing company called ComShare that was in the process of installing a modern Xerox Sigma 7 near the airport in Toronto. The Sigma 7 was a wonderful, highly advanced machine that allowed access to its features remotely. Such access was called time-sharing. If you couldn't afford an in-house machine, you could gain interactive access remotely and pay only for your usage. After ComShare got the Sigma 7 operational in Toronto, our computing students started using it. It was an impressive system.

Time-sharing foreshadowed personal computers and cloud computing. You sat at a terminal consisting of a keyboard and a printer or video display. You dialed the remote computer, not caring where it was located—in a cloud, for all you knew—and you had a powerful resource at your fingertips. The only fly in the ointment at the time was the high cost of communication.

As academic computing grew at WLU, we began to explore the possibility of a small in-house system. A Honeywell 316 was selected in 1971. It was a small minicomputer operated in batch mode. It sported a disc drive the size and shape of a top-loading washing machine with a capacity, astonishing at the time, of fifteen megabytes, a card reader, and a printer. It was installed on the fifth floor of the Central Teaching Building.

It was a modest beginning, but it became a major success. Norm Wagner was one of the early major users, maintaining a database, and the highly successful WLU Stock Market Simulation program was developed on it, all in FORTRAN. We were then joined by a gifted young man, Dave Mathews, to operate the machine. One of his first significant contributions was a modification to the software that reduced the interval between successive jobs from minutes to seconds. It made the machine ideal for the processing of small, card-based student jobs.

Interest in the facility grew. Conrad Winn, in the Department of Sociology, analyzed data using a FORTRAN-based package called SPSS. It soon became obvious that our small Honeywell system could not accommodate SPSS and our thoughts turned to a larger system. In the fall of 1974 students returned to find, installed on the first floor of the Central Teaching Building, a Xerox Sigma 7 and teletype terminal clusters around the campus. Again, Dave Mathews showed great energy and ingenuity in making the Sigma a tremendous success. The choice of the Sigma was obvious because of our earlier encounters through ComShare.

There was fear among some that our relationship with the University of Waterloo might be jeopardized if we acquired a major computer, but the strong support of individuals such as Flora Roy of the English department, Paul Fischer of the bookstore, Conrad Winn, the library's Erich Schultz, Dean Neale Tayler, and President Frank Peters won the day, and the great step was taken. The Sigma 7 served well for ten years, replaced in 1984 by a large Honeywell machine.

As I look back, it's clear that dedicated people kept the machines functioning and made them increasingly user-friendly. Dave Mathews was a significant contributor. Ian Davis developed a wonderfully flexible and ingenious database system used by the library, and Rob Arnold, along with Werner Ullmann, looked after the needs of the Registrar's Office with great innovation and success. Arleen Greenwood put a warm and friendly face on our user interactions for many years, and Carl Langford developed and maintained useful software and doggedly pursued software problems. Stefanie MacKinnon ensured the smooth day-to-day operation of the machine room, and Andrzej Gadomski looked after the far-flung communication system with tremendous energy and great success.

I resigned as director of Computing Services at the end of 1992. After an enriching sabbatical year at the Instituto Tecnológico de Monterrey, Mexico, I returned to full-time teaching in the Department of Physics and Computing until my retirement in 2003.

Chapter 19

Don't Judge a Book by Its Cover
(Or, Peeling the Onion)

BRUCE FOURNIER

IT WAS SUMMER AND I WASN'T TEACHING ANY COURSES. BUT JOHN Banks had to be away, so he asked if I'd cover his third-year organizational behaviour class for him. The topic was role-casting and how our stereotypes and expectations affect how we deal with people.

I'd never seen this class before, so I thought I would use their unfamiliarity with me to "peel the onion." If I did something to provoke a stereotype and shake their expectations, there'd be an additional dimension of learning beyond the chapter in the text and the case study we were to work with that morning.

I'd been painting my house that summer, and my jeans were a riot of colour. I had a worn denim jacket and a pair of workboots my son had worn when he worked on a farm. My poor old cap had gone overboard while we were boating and showed a lot of signs of abuse. I thought that not shaving that day would confuse the image a bit too. For props, I hung a tape measure on my belt and picked up an old clipboard. And I put my text and teaching materials in a red metal toolbox.

I arrived at the classroom a few minutes early. Since the building was quite new, there were often workmen trudging around. I moved around the classroom, appearing to be checking the duplex wall outlets and scribbling notes on my clipboard. The students were very accommodating, moving their chairs out of my way, but generally ignoring me.

At precisely 8:30, class start time, I put my toolbox on the desk at the front of the classroom and asked, "So what are you people all here for?"

Several of the students replied, "We've got a class."

One of them asked, "What are you doing here?" There was a bit of a guffaw.

"They told me I could work in here first thing this morning," I replied. Not a word of a lie here.

"Maybe we should leave," one of the guys near the back of the room offered.

"No, I don't think so," I said.

And then, just as if on cue, a guy wearing a backwards baseball cap suggested, "Why don't you teach us organizational behaviour?" There was a collective snicker all around the class. I snapped opened the latches on my red metal toolbox and took out the first overhead transparency that I had prepared for the class, put it on the projector glass, and turned on the projector.

The next collective was a class-wide sucking in of shock that had the potential to create a low-pressure area capable of bringing rain to southern Ontario for three days. The onion was peeling. The first layer was a big one.

We had a great time laughing about how they'd made assumptions about what a professor should look like and about how they'd assumed that a tradesman wouldn't know anything about organizational behaviour. They conceded that tradesmen, who often work in settings where cooperation and collaboration can mean the difference between life and death, did indeed know a lot about human behaviour in organizations. Then we used the contents of the chapter of the text as a tool for analyzing the case. And two more layers of the onion came off.

Well, it worked this time. It had not worked so well the first time I had tried to peel the onion in a class on role-casting and expectations. I had donned a set of coveralls over my suit and headed for the elevator carrying my red metal toolbox. Being a little embarrassed about my costume, I had my head down as I entered the elevator. I pushed the button for the fifth floor, the door closed and the elevator jerked its way to the third floor in a most alarming fashion. It lurched to a stop and there was complete silence. By silence, I mean that there was no sound of the door opening. More silence.

I pushed the button for Open. Still silence. I pushed the button for the fifth floor again. Silence. Then I pushed the buttons for the other floors. Nothing. Then I pushed the button for Close. That was smart. Silence. There was only one button left that I had not pushed. It was red. By now I was panicking—for two reasons. First, I was trapped in an elevator. Second, if I didn't make it to class within ten minutes, the students would be free to leave. So I pushed the red button.

I was sure they could hear the alarm bell all the way to Toronto. Silence. Then I heard a deep voice rumble up the elevator shaft, "Didn't you read the sign?" Because I entered the elevator with my embarrassed head down, I didn't even see the sign.

"No," I uttered lamely.

"Then you'll just have to wait," boomed the deep voice again.

Silence. Then a bit of muttering from more than one voice. I can't say that the subsequent lurching of the elevator downwards was entirely a relief. The erratic movement was disconcerting. But the prospect of facing the workmen whose labours I had interrupted concerned me as well.

Second floor, the light above the door read Ground Floor. I was headed for the basement, six floors from the destination that I had two minutes to reach. The elevator jerked to a stop. There was a hesitation, and then the door opened. There stood three men in coveralls, with several opened red toolboxes beside them on the floor. I stepped out of the elevator, said "Thank you," and ran for the stairway. Six floors, wearing a suit under a set of coveralls and carrying a toolbox laden with books and notes. My entrance into the classroom was indeed dramatic—I looked like a set of coveralls with a twelve-inch beet on top. I had certainly established a new set of expectations with this class, but not exactly the one I had hoped for. I may also have set a record for ascending six flights of stairs in the Central Teaching Building as well.

Maybe the onion approach was inspirational. A red onion, perhaps.

Chapter 20

Making Canadian History

BARRY GOUGH

$\mathcal{G}$ ARRIVED IN WATERLOO IN 1972 ON THE SAME DAY THAT THE NDP swept into power in British Columbia. It was a propitious moment in my passage. I knew of Kitchener-Waterloo only by reputation, my pianist mother recommending the musical creativity of my destination highly. The financial stability of the region and its diversity in the economic sphere were, as advertised, self-evident on my arrival. I recall that first night, with its languid late-August air—a relief from the searing heat of the afternoon—and I awaited the next day with a keen sense of duty. It was time to get to work.

At my interview the previous February I had been struck by the collegiality of faculty and staff alike. The students had gone out of their way to parade the fine quality of their instructors. We chatted in the Torque Room, then the heart of conversation and friendship. Later, Erich Shultz, the university librarian, showed me the stacks, notably the history shelves, where I was pleased to find all the great jewels in my fields of interest, lovingly recommended for purchase by historian Welf Heick and others who cared about library acquisitions. When exiting one university (Western Washington University, in this instance), it is always wise to see what books familiar to you are to be found at the destination institution.

I attended the faculty meeting, held upstairs in what was then the Central Teaching Building—incredibly spartan in its cinder-block construction. The room where we met possessed a vaulted view to the north and west over the hundred-acre farms that stood out towards St. Jacobs and beyond—the towns on the margins, as it were, little entities unto themselves—and well worth exploring over the coming years in the company of new friends Gerry Noonan, Bob McCauley, and Edna Staebler. Each year we traversed a new circuit, perhaps looking in on a buggy works, exploring some artist's aerie, or examining some vintage public house in deepest Wellesley.

Our commuter students came from many of these locales, and our student body was peppered with elementary school teachers from those towns finishing their bachelor's degrees. We had a strong representation from the Celtic fringe of Ontario—Lambton and Elgin counties across to the Bruce and Grey areas—which much later gave way to urbanites trekking west from Mississauga and Toronto. This, then, was my new Canada. It was altogether different from my home port of Victoria, B.C., the world at its oceanic portal. Here in southern Ontario the economic engines were different: agriculture, financial services, insurance, manufacturing of all sorts, and academia, all living in harmony, though many of those companies had sold their operations to American corporations—another side of the story.

Democratic institutions had marked the community since the 1830s, underlying the egalitarianism I sensed day to day. The burgher class of old Waterloo County still existed, though many summered in Muskoka and wintered in Florida, timing their return to their native hearth just in time to sign their annual tax statements and keep their OHIP in force.

When I arrived, the university had about two thousand students and a commensurately small faculty. Inaccurately labelled "Last Chance U," it had some of the brightest students imaginable, including one of them, Sean Conway, my teaching assistant, who was elected to the Ontario legislature, served as a cabinet minister, and now teaches at Queen's University. On inquiry, I discovered that many of our graduates who had become teachers in Ontario schools had recommended WLU to their students. A fine tribute.

There and then we developed the hugely successful annual history teachers conferences held conveniently on one of the teachers' professional development days. Drawing high school teachers from southwestern Ontario, we brought them up to date on the burning issues of our profession—and shared good collegiality as co-workers in the history business. We worked closely with the history teachers in Waterloo Region, some of whom had key connections to WLU, notably Harold Russell, Bill Weiler, and Jack Sinkins. The conference kept WLU front and centre in the minds of high school teachers as a place dedicated to good instruction. They repaid us by sending us their best students. My colleagues shared in the enthusiasm of this enterprise. It continues to this day.

My past travels and education in three countries had given me a strategic advantage in what I set out to do in the university. I had seen Canada from the American perspective and especially from the British and Commonwealth perspective. I had worked to advance Canadian Studies in the United States and been an architect of the Canadian–American Center at Western Washington University. Driven from a tenured spot by strife and discord there, I wondered if I could make a mark among the more somnolent colleagues whose ranks I had joined. Among the early lessons to be learnt was that martini diplomacy counted for little, pre-position papers were worthless, and opposition to change was likely to raise its weary head. Grandstanding in faculty meetings made for good theatre, I found, and I refused to engage in that ploy. Before long I found myself on the top senate executive committees. With the financial papers laid out before me, I marvelled at how so much was done with so little—a WLU secret.

The era itself was preoccupied with anti-American sentiment, with political and academic careers being made on Canada as allegedly an American branch plant and much else. I refused then, as I do now, to play that game: to me history was a means of displaying the Canadian past, warts and all. Canadians needed to tell their stories, to celebrate their diversities, and, against the odds, to show their common past and purpose. Thus it was that I found myself immersed in founding a Canadian Studies program. Tom Symons, president of Trent University, came to give us a hand, as did Bruce Hodgins, a graduate of WLU and an unabashed proponent of Canadian Studies, particularly with a Commonwealth twist. Soon other departments volunteered talents—notably English, Geography, and Anthropology. Our students held the program in high regard and before long we were graduating students with a major or minor in the area.

The times favoured me. I had been tutored in British Empire history. Now I was seeing it recording its last chapters in Canadian history, with a twist. The two houses of the Canadian Parliament voted for a joint resolution to patriate the British North America Act. Along with this came an amending formula and a Charter of Rights and Freedoms, both revolutionary instruments of statecraft. At the time, this unsettling step sparked heated debate. To clear the air and to provide a means of informed discussion, I introduced a course on the history of the Canadian constitution. This ran parallel to another of my favorites at the time, a history of Canadian external affairs. Some of my colleagues scratched their heads, thinking that poring over dusty old documents about arcane constitutional matters was the nearest thing to watching paint dry.

However, the local CTV affiliate took notice of what we were up to and started reporting on it. There was, after all, much unfinished business: first the Meech Lake Accord and later the equally ill-fated Charlottetown Accord. John Redekop of Political Science and I drew up a report card on Canadian public figures of the time, a national attention-getter that was far more effective than another Gallup poll. Some of my colleagues in Political Science and many majors in that subject were stalwarts in the study of the history of Canadian external affairs. The companion course on the constitution was full of would-be diplomats and consuls, some who lived their dream and went on to important diplomatic positions.

Looking back on those years, I was immensely fortunate to be living through times of great and significant change in Canada. The Vietnam War with all its horrid after-effects was leaving us at last. There were, naturally, preoccupations with multiculturalism and with Quebec as a distinct society (which historians worth their salt already credited). But it was of powerful importance to me to have a front-row seat on history as it unfolded and to use the classroom as a way to articulate the differences, the conflicts, and the compromises.

These constitutional eruptions had exposed gender inequalities and, particularly to my interests, the appalling state of Canada's Aboriginal peoples (Indians, Métis, and Inuit). My book Gunboat Frontier (1984) examined the cross-cultural relations between official forces on the Pacific coast and the various First Nations—Haida, Tsimsian, Salish, and others. Having first given myself a crash course in anthropology, a subject

that had escaped me as an undergraduate, I determined to introduce a
course on the history of First Nations in Canada—two courses, in fact,
one on Eastern Woodlands and the North; the other, the Prairie and
Pacific West. This drew in many anthropology and archaeology students
and brought me closer to colleagues in those departments, respectively
and notably Laird Christie and Dean Knight. I discovered a vast network
of like-minded scholars in nearby universities and, before long, out of our
discussions and mutual interest was born the Laurier Conference on
Ethnohistory. It was backed by the Museum of Canadian Civilization, Eth-
nology Branch, which published our work in its Mercury Series.

From all these interrelated teaching experiences I developed my own
thesis about Canadian history: Canada was a new version of the British
Empire in North America, with all the trappings of imperial power,
devolved authority, and even instruments of control, notably the Indian
Act. For myself and my students, that a Charter of Rights and Freedoms
and an amending formula had been brought in at the time of the patri-
ation of the British North America Act, effective April 17, 1982, was a
remarkable progression. In after years I watched the birthdates on the registrar's lists provided with each class, and, sure enough, before too long
the first Canadians born with no obstacles of imperial impediment were
sitting in my classroom. I recall the moment and proclaimed its importance. There was no return to empire now.

Early on I found a willing partner in Norman Wagner of the School
of Religion and Culture, which he had been instrumental in establishing,
and a pioneer in the publishing of scholarly works.[1] His efforts came to
fruition in the formation of Wilfrid Laurier University Press, which in my
opinion is Laurier's greatest gift to the world of learning. He was an
unusual figure in an institution of higher learning, remarkably creative
in his progressive thinking and his knack for getting things done. Before
moving on to the presidency of the University of Calgary, on the advice
of a small team of which I was a member he brought real direction to
research on campus by introducing a system of research grants, including no-strings-attached initiatory research grants, to encourage faculty
to embark on new enterprises as well as to complete old projects. Before

---

1 Norman Wagner, "Scholars as Publishers: A New Paradigm," *Scholarly Publishing* 7
   (January 1976): 101–12.

long there was much talk in the hallways concerning the relative merits of good teaching and service to the university or publication of a few articles compared with the publication of a leading book. These developments reflected national and international change in academia, and, not surprisingly, there were growing pains.

In 1973 an organization of inspired individuals known on campus as the Interdisciplinary Committee on Modernization and Development invited me to speak. As my topic I chose "Canada and the American Empire," a subject then much in the news and one touched on in my book *Canada* (1975) published in the Modern Nations in Historical Perspective series edited by my mentor Robin Winks of Yale. This was my first exposure to what became the Interdisciplinary Research Seminar, whose files are in the Laurier archives. Ahead of the times in the promoting of interdisciplinary, multi-disciplinary, and cross-disciplinary research, the dozen or so sages who sat round that great board table in the bowels of the Laurier library met monthly to discuss subjects that no single university department in the humanities or social sciences would dare contemplate. Statisticians, demographers, sociologists, social workers, and others met to talk about the topic of the day.

How refreshing this was, particularly inasmuch as there was no time for this in the History department save for corridor chats and gossip. The seminar published an Occasional Papers series and some conference papers. Like much else in the exploratory line, the seminar transmogrified into some other sort of academic configuration. I devoted about twenty years to the seminar, ably assisted by Toivo Miljan, Bill Marr, Douglas McCready, John Jenkins, and others. Of course, there were doubters, but I was pleased to see how new formations came along, Arctic communities' research, for example, and a rejuvenated Canadian Studies cluster.

Thirty-three years is a good long time to work in one institution of higher learning, and when I look back on it now I can sense the pulse of the place and its excitement, also its changing moods and its periodic worries. Of growing pains there had been more than enough. Many faculty and staff moved on to what they thought would be greener pastures. But those who persisted possessed a stout-hearted nature. I saw the insecurities expressed by the faculty give way to a more assured sense of purpose, individually and collectively. From a personal perspective, it seems that rather than go chasing for the world, it came to me, and at the end of my years there, when it was time to go, I had made the university my own. I then knew that it could never disown me, or I it. Now that's tenure.

Chapter 21

From Poverty to War:
An Historian's Odyssey

TERRY COPP

$\mathcal{M}$Y ASSOCIATION WITH WILFRID LAURIER UNIVERSITY BEGAN in the spring of 1975 when I accepted an appointment as associate professor in the Department of History. The decision to leave Montreal, where I had grown up, gone to school and university, and begun a teaching career at McGill and Concordia was not made lightly. My research was firmly focused on the history of Montreal and its large working-class population. After completing *The Anatomy of Poverty: The Condition of the Working Class in Montreal 1897–1929* (1974), the first title in the new Canadian Social History Series, I began research on the Great Depression years and the economic boom of the 1940s and 1950s.

The move to Laurier was motivated by a family desire to leave city life behind and to teach in a smaller, less anonymous university. We happily settled in the Elora area. My research continued to focus on Montreal with the publication of articles on municipal welfare in the Depression, public health issues, and especially the rise of industrial unions. I initially taught courses in the history of French Canada and labour. There were very few M.A. students available to work with, but my fourth-year undergraduate seminar was full of bright, energetic students; so we adapted the work I had been doing on Montreal to Kitchener and produced a volume of essays published as *Industrial Unionism in Kitchener: Essays by Students at Wilfrid Laurier University* (1976). A number of honours B.A. theses followed on the development of unions in other towns in central Ontario. It was this kind of research that first brought Brantford and its decaying industrial core to my attention. Years later, while exploring the Grand River watershed with my wife, Linda, who was preparing an art exhibit *A Year on the Grand*, I returned to the city and was inspired to make the first contacts that led President Bob Rosehart to initiate Laurier Brantford.

My interest in the impact of international industrial unions in the 1940s and their "demonstration effect" on wages to non-unionized employees was based on persuasive evidence that escaping the poverty trap required worker organization as well as economic growth. During the war the ratio of income between salaried employees and hourly wage earners had shifted dramatically toward higher wages, and the Family Allowance had made a significant impact on income distribution. This was the approach I brought to a book titled *Working People* that Desmond Morton and I published in 1980.

Desmond remains a good friend and colleague. He joins us each year on the Cleghorn Battlefield Study Tour, but we approached labour history from very different directions. He was interested in the Co-operative Commonwealth Federation–New Democratic Party and its policies, not the North American labour-market approach I employed. Des and I also had very different opinions about unionization of professional workers in government and semi-private sectors. When the campaign to unionize faculty at Laurier began, I publicly opposed certification, arguing that the adversarial nature of collective bargaining would replace collegial governance, weakening senates and councils. I suppose it was ironic that a faculty member with an honorary life membership in an international union and an active membership in ACTRA—the Alliance of Canadian Cinema, Television and Radio Artists—should speak out against unionization, but for me it was a matter of principle. I could not possibly view well-paid faculty as workers needing the protections of collective bargaining. Both Des and I were also out of step with the new labour history of the 1980s that celebrated working-class culture and offered a Marxist critique of welfare capitalism. There did not seem to be much future for either of us in such a field.

I was therefore open to the suggestion that I abandon the archives of the International Union of Electrical Workers in New Jersey, the United Auto Workers' records in Detroit, and the delights of the Canadian Labour Department in Hull for something completely different: the experience of the Canadian army in the Second World War. The late Robert Vogel, my mentor, sometime colleague, and friend, was completing his second term as dean of Arts at McGill and his administrative leave coincided with my first Laurier sabbatical. We decided to work together studying the military operations to clear the approaches to the port of Antwerp in October 1944. Bob would search the German sources and deal with the broad strategic issues and I would attempt a from-the-ground-up study of the ways in which the Canadian soldiers had organized themselves to win a crucial battle.

As a social and labour historian I had always tried to use oral history to help understand the context of events, so I naturally initiated a series of interesting and deeply rewarding interviews with veterans. When writing about Montreal or Kitchener I had walked the streets in an attempt to understand the built environment; so my wife, Linda, and I made the first of many trips to the European battlefields. It did not take long to learn that a detailed knowledge of battlefield terrain is fundamental to military history.

University of Western Ontario historian Jack Hyatt, an old and valued friend, once told his graduate seminar that when Copp became a military historian, the workers became soldiers and the bosses became generals, and it was pretty clear where Copp's sympathies lay. There is some truth in this. My interviews with those who had been junior officers, privates, or NCOs in 1944 confirmed my view that the war was fought and won at the sharp end by ordinary young men challenged to do extraordinary things.

Military history was not a popular subject in universities or Canadian publishing in 1981. After an initial article in the *Journal of Canadian Studies*, Bob and I decided to self-publish a series of illustrated books telling the story of the Canadians in Normandy and northwest Europe. We called it a "new reading" of the primary evidence in that it tried to understand events as they happened without benefit of hindsight. My colleagues in the Laurier History department, who had hired a social-labour historian, found themselves instead with a tenured professor who taught a heavily enrolled course on the Second World War and drew graduate students to study the Canadian experience of war.

The five volumes of the Maple Leaf Route series (1983–1988) actually sold well and even made money. The series won the first C.P. Stacey Prize and was well reviewed internationally. The connection between social and military history was even more evident in *Battle Exhaustion: Soldiers and Psychiatrists in the Canadian Army* (1990), written with Bill McAndrew, which dealt with combat stress, and in *The Brigade* (1992), which included an analysis of the socio-economic background of a sample of 1,100 soldiers killed in action.

The 1980s were an exciting decade at Laurier. Arthur Stephen, through his award-winning films and other initiatives on behalf of Laurier, created an image of what the university could be, and President John Weir provided the leadership that made it all possible. By 1991 Canadian military history was well established at Laurier and we joined the circle of major Canadian universities receiving a National Defence grant to finance a research centre under the Security and Defence Forum program. A new journal, *Canadian Military History*, was established and the first international military history colloquium, now in its twentieth year, was begun.

Upon my retirement in 2004 the university offered me a continuing appointment as director of the Laurier Centre for Military Strategic and Disarmament Studies. The Centre continues to encourage research and publication, especially in the field of Canadian military history. With the support of the university and individuals like John and Pattie Cleghorn, the Centre publishes battlefield guidebooks and much else. One current project involves the translation and annotation of the official German history of the Great War and a parallel project making the official German medical history of 1914–18 available to English-language readers.

My own work on Canada in the Second World War culminated in the publication of two books, *Fields of Fire: The Canadians in Normandy* (2003) and *Cinderella Army: The Canadians in Northwest Europe* (2006). A new book, *Combat Stress: The Commonwealth Experience*, developed with my former Laurier student Dr. Mark Humphries, will appear in 2011.

Chapter 22

Multiculturalism at WLU:
Opening to the Wider World

JOSEPHINE C. NAIDOO

MARRIAGE TO JAMES LESLIE, A TORONTONIAN WHOM I HAD MET when we were both graduate students at the University of Illinois–Urbana-Champaign, brought me to Waterloo, first to St. Jerome's College in 1964 and then to Waterloo Lutheran University in 1969, and to teaching and research that went quite beyond what I had ever envisaged upon arrival.

It was a university much different in size and especially in character from the present Wilfrid Laurier, more specifically in diversity of faculty and students and in horizons and areas of study. Historically, it was the Trudeau era. Changes in policies regarding immigration (1962), bilingualism (1969), and multiculturalism (1971) were making Canada a microcosm of the world. In the spirit of Sir Wilfrid Laurier and his legacy of respect for "difference," new attitudes of acceptance, tolerance—indeed excitement—about global peoples, their cultures, religions, philosophies, and histories were becoming part of the Canadian scene.

It was in this fertile multicultural environment that my interests in cross-cultural psychology, race relations, minority women (especially of South Asian ancestry), indigenous peoples, and intercultural conflict resolution first took root. My thirty years in the Department of Psychology were undergirded and often inspired by the university's growing aspirations for excellence in teaching, research, and international visibility and by the resources offered to back up those aspirations. Also important to my teaching and research was the intellectual interaction among

113

the faculty and with the local multicultural community and, later, the national and international communities.

In the wake of the reports of the royal commissions on bilingualism and biculturalism (1969) and the status of women (1970), and given the early presence of women from India and other parts of South Asia in Waterloo region, I undertook a field study of this population, on which basically no empirical work had been conducted. My moving beyond the boundaries of strict behavioralism to an interdisciplinary approach raised some academic eyebrows; within the South Asian community the study was perceived by some as intrusive. Today, of course, such research is commonplace worldwide.

Along the same line, I began to teach a graduate course in the M.A. program in social-community psychology entitled "Multicultural Processes in Canadian Perspective" and served on many thesis and dissertation committees where the research had a multicultural focus. In 1987 I was invited to join the Doctor of Social Work program as a cognate faculty member.

Broadening my research horizons further, in 1997 I spent a year at the de-racialized University of KwaZulu-Natal in Durban, South Africa, where I undertook a study of the traumatic experiences of minority Asian Indians during the apartheid era. In 2001, as a guest of our daughter, Michèle Leslie, then a physician at Baffin Regional Hospital, Iqaluit, Nunavut Territory, I had the rare opportunity to meet the Inuit people of Nunavut and to become acquainted with their artistic expression, language, institutions, and problems of settlement and adaptation. An in-depth study of the empirical, historical, and anecdotal literature on the Inuit yielded a presentation at an international cross-cultural psychology conference in historic Xi'an, China (2004) and then an article (2008). At the same time, various collaborative studies of South Asian migration in global and historical context facilitated my contributions to an encyclopedia of the Indian diaspora spearheaded by the National University of Singapore (2006) and as invited editor of a special issue of the *Journal of Psychology and Developing Societies* on the Indian diaspora (2005).

My most stirring life experience took place away from the campus, serving as an election observer in the first democratic elections in South Africa while on sabbatical leave there in 1993–94. I was born and raised in apartheid South Africa. The pain of fifty years of repressive legislation, enforced racial separation, and ethnic cleansing for millions of non-white South Africans is almost beyond description. That year I was based at the segregated Indian University, engaged in research on Indian and African students. As the advent of democracy approached, all the universities commenced the arduous task of "de-racialization" of their student and faculty populations. Witnessing the crumbling of an evil political system and ideology and experiencing the triumph of the people is engraved in my memory.

From among many rewarding professional experiences three stand out for me:

1. Serving as a member of a federal task force that studied the mental health of immigrants and refugees (1986–88); the report of the task force (1988) has helped to sensitize the health system to the cultural needs of Canadian newcomers.
2. Serving as secretary-general of the International Association for Cross-Cultural Psychology (1994–96); the close interaction with researchers and the mentoring of students around the globe remains a valued experience.
3. Attending a meeting of the South African Psychological Association while on sabbatical leave in Durban in 1993. Political change from apartheid to democracy was on the horizon. The focus of the meeting was the unification of liberal and conservative branches of the association, split for many years. To my surprise, the president of the Unification Committee asked me to stand up. He told the assembly that it was my application for membership in the association in the late 1950s—the first from a "black" psychologist—that had triggered the split, now in the process of historic reconciliation. The announcement was greeted with applause.

To add a footnote to that event, at the time of my application I was a lecturer in psychology at Pius XII University College, located in Roma in the British Protectorate of Basutoland. (Today, the country is independent Lesotho, and the college was replaced by the National University of Lesotho.) In rejecting my request for membership in the South African Psychological Association, the president of the association, the well-known Dr. Simon Biesheuvel, wrote that "owing to social circumstances in South Africa, the Association cannot accept your application."

As inveterate participants in international conferences know, conference organizers invariably arrange visits to museums, art displays, architecture, and people. Contributing to my cross-cultural research and
awareness were four memorable experiences from over 30 countries visited during my WLU days.

New Zealand, 1988. From the University of Waikato in the city of
Hamilton we spent a weekend with Maori people in their *marae*, their
sacred space. We cross-cultural psychologists from forty-four countries
shared in Maori communal living, interacted with Maori people, and
listened to presentations about Maori issues and problems by Maori
leaders and government officials.

China, 2004. We visited the Qin Shi Huang Mausoleum, displaying
the Terra Cotta warriors of the first emperor of the Qin Dynasty, a short
distance from the historic city of Xi'an, in Shaanxi Province, where our
conference was held. According to UNESCO, this marvel of an ancient
civilization is perhaps the most significant archeological find of the twentieth century.

Japan, 1990. Our conferences were held in the historic city of Nara,
famous for its deer park, and Kyoto, famous for its golden pagoda. After
the conferences, I fulfilled a longtime yearning to experience firsthand
something of the horror of the dropping of the first atomic bombs on
Hiroshima and Nagasaki. The museum at Hiroshima recreates a very
realistic scenario of the painful sights and sounds of that terrible day
in 1945. By contrast, the Peace Garden, with its message of transcend-
ing the inhumanity of which humans are capable to attain a greater
peace, love, and compassion, will always remain deeply embedded in
my consciousness.

India, 1980. I risked missing my plane in order to make a quick taxi
trip to see the famed Sun Temple at Konarak, a few miles from
Bhubaneswar in the state of Orissa, the site of the international conference I was attending. Erected in the thirteenth century over 16 years and
with the labour of 1,200 artisans, the temple was conceived as a chariot
for the Sun God, Surya. Three impressive chlorite images of Surya are
aligned to catch the sun at dawn, noon, and sunset. The immense complex, today protected as a UNESCO World Heritage Site, includes gigan-
tic carvings and sculptures of elephants, horses, and chariot wheels. Also
portrayed are erotic images of entwined couples. I brought home sculp-

tures of two voluptuous nude females preening themselves, a gift for my husband.

Looking back, I recall how Canada's need of doctors, engineers, and other well-educated professionals was expanding. Canada opened its doors to refugees—Ugandan Asians, the Hmong people of Laos, Tibetans, Eritreans, and ethnic Vietnamese. Previously, immigrants had hailed primarily from European countries; Canada was a "white man's country." My own studies indicated that mainstream Canadians tended to reject ethnic dress, ethnic foods, turbans, nose rings, and the *tikka* (dot) on the foreheads of Indian women. A spirit of exclusion of "difference"— that such newcomers did not "belong"—permeated the institutions of our society, filtering also into university communities. In this regard I recall with admiration and appreciation the progressive stance taken by the late Dr. Neale Tayler, vice-president: academic at the time, and the administration generally. Today, forty years later, the barriers have diminished, but they continue to be a challenge, right now especially with regard to Islam and Muslims.

As I perceive it, both my own world view and that of WLU have changed over my near half-century association with it. From a small university with a relatively homogenous faculty and student body, WLU has expanded and blossomed. Today it offers courses and programs that reflect the diversity, complexity, and rapidly changing character of our contemporary world. I am excited to see offerings on international migration, aboriginal peoples, and global issues, indeed a very popular Department of Global Studies. The WLU community has become more cosmopolitan, representing more accurately Canada's changing demographics.

At the university bearing his name, the spirit of Sir Wilfrid Laurier, with his deep commitment to "the cause of unity, concord and harmony among the citizens of this country," has made impressive progress toward achieving those aspirations of the sixties and seventies. The future holds dynamic promise. We celebrate!

Chapter 23

Reflections: One Person's Perspective

BILL MARR

 CAME TO WATERLOO LUTHERAN UNIVERSITY IN 1970 AS A LECTURER in the Department of Economics, School of Business and Economics, and retired in 2009 as a professor in that same department in what had become Wilfrid Laurier University. Over almost four decades I have seen as well as participated in many changes at the "old" and the "new" WLU. Yet some things have remained the same.

In 1970, Waterloo Lutheran University was indeed a small university in the Ontario university system, and the small size was reflected in the number of full-time faculty in both the Department of Economics and the Department of Business; as I recall there were about seven faculty in each of the two departments. Gatherings of faculty, friends, and spouses, usually held at the home of the dean or the chair, were common. The department went for dinner in September as one way to welcome new members to the department, and the president of the university had a dinner for all faculty members and staff at about the same time. There was still a marks meeting which all full-time faculty attended to discuss situations where a student might need a mark or two changed to continue on or to graduate. There were also various other meetings that included faculty from across the university. Convocation ceremonies were held at Kitchener Memorial Auditorium, with most faculty members in attendance.

All of this meant that we got to know faculty members and staff from all departments and areas of the university. As one personal example, when I arrived in August of 1970, my student awards and scholarships funding had all ended earlier that year; monies that I earned from teach-ing introductory economics at King's College, University of Western Ontario, had been spent and my first WLU paycheque was not due until September 18. Meanwhile, food had to be purchased and rent had to be paid. I asked John Weir, who was the chair of the Department of Econom-ics, if he would talk with the comptroller to see if she would give me an advance on that first paycheque. She did, and my family and I could eat and pay the rent. Would such still happen today?

Coming to Waterloo Lutheran in 1970 was an ideal career choice for me. In 1962, when I was looking for a university to attend as an under-graduate, Waterloo Lutheran University had the reputation among high school students in Ontario as "Last Chance U." I do not know if that was justified, but by 1970 that was changing. While WLU was first and fore-most a "teaching institution," the new faculty members wanted to engage in research as well. We had received our Ph.D.s from research-oriented graduate programs and we had research agendas based, in the first instance, on our dissertations. We wanted to be in the classroom, but we also wanted to give papers at conferences and to publish books and arti-cles. WLU changed in response to these expanded and multi-dimen-sional interests. For the most part, WLU over my career provided the resources and encouragement to enable me to do both teaching and research. Is that still the situation?

In my thirty-nine years at WLU I tried to maintain a balance among teaching, research, and service to the university community and beyond. Somewhere I had read that full-time faculty members should allocate about 40% of their time to teaching, 40% to research, and 20% to serv-ice. So that is what I tried to do, with one small caveat. I never regarded those percentages as a prescription for each year of working life but, rather, for some longer time frame, such as a decade. Over a decade, I tried to observe that 40–40–20 percentage allocation, but in any one year more or less time was devoted to each of those three activities. In the 1970s I allocated more time to teaching; for a new faculty member that meant six one-term courses, including several first-time preparations. In the 1980s I allocated more time to research that was well under way, to research grants, and employing students as research assistants. In the 1990s I allocated more time to service, as assistant dean of Graduate Stud-ies and Research and associate director of Instructional Development—

but I also continued to be active in research and teaching, with a lower teaching load because of those other responsibilities. The 2000s probably reflected the closest balance among teaching, research, and service. WLU was a good place to be; there was always a great deal of flexibility in one's time allocation among those three functions, and colleagues, administrators, and staff provided support. Is that still the situation?

WLU has an official motto—*Veritas Omnia Vincit*—but for me personally it was *People Before Programs*. The individual was more important than the particular program of study a student happened to be in, more important than the particular department or area of the university a faculty member or staff member happened to be in. Over my almost four decades, it was possible to get to know many students beyond a number on a marks sheet, although that became harder as class sizes grew in my later years. I was fortunate to serve on many committees, boards, and task forces over my career, which brought me into contact with faculty members and staff from across WLU. I came to appreciate their needs and concerns, and to know them as people and not just as names. People—students, staff, faculty members—were "of the university" rather than just of a particular program of study or a particular department or area. Is that the situation now that WLU is so much larger? Perhaps faculty members now will know just as many students, staff, and faculty as I did, but they will come from a narrower spectrum of the university, which may reduce the possibility of developing common interests and objectives.

There is a saying that attempts to put one's life and work into some perspective. It is actually a question: *Do you live to work, or do you work to live?* I have tried to work to live, but I must admit that there were times over my career at WLU when work more or less took over for a period of time and I found that I was living to work. Is it possible now at WLU to work to live?

I would invite readers with ties to WLU, past and present, to reflect on my reflections, compare them with their own, and then perhaps ask themselves the questions that came to me as I looked back over four decades at the university that was so central in my life.

Chapter 24

Old English, Old Norse, Dr. Roy (and Bishop Berkeley): Fifty Years at WLU

PETER C. ERB

W–L–U: FOR WHAT I WOULD ESTIMATE TO BE A MINUSCULE MINORITY the initials still stand for Waterloo Lutheran University, even though now nearly forty years have passed since that name became history, and even though the institution remained under that name for a mere thirteen years.

In 1962, the third year after Waterloo Lutheran University came into being, I enrolled at this new university as an honours English and Latin student, following Grade 13, the fifth year of Ontario's high school system, the final examinations of which were marked anonymously in Toronto and from which students could proceed to a general B.A. (three years) or to a four-year honours degree in one of the disciplines of the time. The buildings then were few. In addition to some houses (in one of which I rented a room) there were the Arts Building, Willison Hall, and Clara Conrad Hall. Two years earlier there had appeared on the campus the first president of this new-but-not-so-new creation, William J. Villaume, who remained only six years but, in a sense, marked the whole of its existence hitherto, embodying as he did Lutheranism and its presence on the campus for almost sixty years at that point. The eventful, often conflicted years that followed epitomized to a large degree the shifting nature of a liberal arts education in a university with a name like Waterloo Lutheran in the Canada of the time and, to some extent, the final upshot of the years that followed. These musings are something of a minority report on those "Lutheran" years, with the caveat that in what follows this non-Lutheran uses "Lutheran" as a broad signifier of elements I deem important in the Canadian academic tradition.

It is commonplace now to ignore the thirteen years when there was a Waterloo Lutheran University or, in the case of the present centenary celebration, to judge it as a small part of the whole. But six decades—1911–73—on Albert Street allow more than that, and the almost forty years of life on the part of Waterloo Lutheran Seminary running alongside that of Wilfrid Laurier University require that one revisit this earlier period.

One year after my graduation from the honours English program, I had returned to Waterloo Lutheran University for one year, 1966–67, to teach English 10, a pre-university course that was part of an arrangement that allowed those without a regular high school degree to take four courses and then to enter the regular degree program. The year was initially designed to aid those who wished to qualify for admission to the seminary, but it had become a means for numerous students, far from the seminary program, to enter the university itself. There was no great concern about such an arrangement at the time. Only a few years prior, aspiring teachers had been able to attend one year at teachers' college following Grade 12 and then teach grade school, followed by two summer sessions that gained them entrance to the regular teaching workforce.

In 1970, having completed my licentiate at the Pontifical Institute of Medieval Studies in Toronto, I returned to the university part-time, as a philologist, teaching Latin, Old English, Old Norse, Old High German ("old" being my entrée, it seemed), upgrading my position to full-time the year following, naively thinking that two universities in the small city of Waterloo would continue, one secular and one religious. Two years later, in 1973, I left WLU to become the director of the Schwenkfelder Library in Pennsburg, Pennsylvania. It was a one-year leave of absence; I didn't know whether I would return. The leave was supported by Flora Roy (1912–2008), chair of the English department. I did return, teaching ten more years in the Department of English and thereafter in the Department of Religion and Culture for another twenty-four.

Upon returning in 1974 I found an institution with a conservative Evangelical replacing the former Lutheran as president and a university named (so it seemed) with the primary intention of saving the initials for its winning football team: Wilfrid Laurier University. The change that had taken place in that year away constituted more than a change in name. The new name signified a change, attendant upon public funding, in hiring of faculty, in areas of study and specializations, in teaching, research, and publication. It took a year or two until the university chaplain departed. This was, one might say, inevitable. "The School of Religion and Culture" (SORAC) continued as a catchword for some years to link seminary to university in the transition from "Lutheran" to "Laurier." Under the umbrella of SORAC, the university department worked as one faculty with the seminary, meeting monthly to do business, to choose and plan courses together for the next year, then adjourning to lunch at Aarne Siirala's, preceded by discussion of a paper in progress. But by the mid-1980s even this had for the most part ceased, for the most part with few regrets. Whatever lingering allegiance there had been on campus to Paul Tillich's aphorism that "Religion is the substance of culture, culture the form of religion" was forgotten or patronized.

I do not mean to disparage the teaching "about" religion that necessarily characterizes religious studies departments in provincial universities in a multicultural society. I lived by that axiom (and fruitfully so, I believe) while teaching in the Religion and Culture department for a quarter of a century. But always present to me as I taught was the example set by Dr. Flora Roy at the time when she was the longest-serving faculty member at WLU: Waterloo Lutheran University, Wilfrid Laurier University, and their predecessor Waterloo College. For me she embodied the "culture" of Tillich's aphorism (and therefore some of the "substance"): a keeping faith with a tradition committed to students, to teaching, and to broad and deep learning that characterized the ethos and traditions of Waterloo College and Waterloo Lutheran University at their best.

One day in the early 1960s that I recall vividly was not an uncommon experience for us students. Dr. Roy was swarmed by a group of undergraduates. The student activity ("buzz," in later lingo) that she inspired was much the same from one day to the next: a barrage of questions seeking answers, with only the questions changing. In this case, the event was initiated by a George Berkeley dialogue studied in class that day, and at the height of the chatter one of the group loudly insisted: "It's true, it's true."

"Ah," Dr. Roy responded, "but 'you know' ... 'you know'.... It might not be so much true as simply beautiful."

And after a brief pause, she shifted her ever-present wicker basket from one arm to the other and walked away to a goal unknown perhaps even to herself. Whether that goal was ever reached, I do not know, but I continue to believe that it was manifested in the next student or colleague, anxious to discover what work of world literature, directly relevant to a question at hand, would appear, not without a little searching and shuffling, from her seemingly bottomless basket.

The "dialogue" that engaged students that day had not appeared on their class syllabus—there was seldom a relationship between Dr. Roy's never-completed syllabus (what syllabus there was before such were demanded) and her classroom monologues. The Berkeley reference had come to students' attention in one of her many and lengthy asides. So important were the asides that some listeners marked off the upper eighth of their notepads with a heavy black line, recording all "facts" above the line, leaving the lower, larger part free for Dr. Roy's rambling historical, philosophical, and literary reflections, and those many koanesque adages that slipped regularly and without warning from between (yes, "between") the synapses of a cultural memory as bottomless as her wicker basket.

"You know ..." was her utterance and hers alone, but it never formulated closure. Inevitably, an ironic pause followed—a pause that enveloped every attentive, graced, and knowing young disciple in a strikingly open *gnosis*. Dr. Roy's "you" was always inclusive, even when the student (or faculty member) addressed had no idea (as was almost always the case) of what was being said. Many were called and not a few chosen.

"You know ..."—and then a pause. As a student or colleague, "you" always did "know," whether "you" grasped the implications of her statement or not. Certainty was never on offer with Dr. Roy. That was the point of her cryptic comment on the central figure of her scholarship, the good, true, and beautiful Bishop Berkeley. As one of the editors of a collection of essays later compiled in her honour would put it:

> Berkeley conceived a Utopian vision of an educational institution, "designed to teach mankind the most refined luxury, to raise the mind to its due perfection, and to give it a taste for those entertainments which afford the richest transport." This sort of description had become a sort of cliché.... Yet as almost anyone who is engaged in the academic

profession will acknowledge, there are distinguished spirits who will rise calmly and easily above the petty routine of workaday life and invoke with supreme efficiency an approximation of the academic ideals of Bishop Berkeley. Everyone who knows Dr. Roy, furthermore, will recognize immediately that to place her in this exclusive company is no mere flattering and meaningless overstatement.[1]

The sort of knowledge in which she revelled was never presented as truth or some transmissible information—gained from an authoritative source and wielded authoritatively thereafter, not even that of the good bishop (or of the revered professor). Her "you know" included a freely given wealth of knowledge and much more: it was an invitation into active *knowing*—into the intellectual life in which "you" were formed, together with many another "you," in which "you" participated and were attracted with ever more certitude by the beautiful.

Some have commented that, without Dr. Roy, Wilfrid Laurier University would not have survived the onslaught of Ontario's technological sixties. Rumour has it that she never travelled University Avenue between Albert and Westmount streets, so as not to pass by the University of Waterloo. If fact underlies this rumour, one needs to keep in mind her observation that "fact" (as she once pointed out) is based on the Latin word "composed." In any event it may be another of the loveable myths, maintained with regularity even by those who support the work of both universities and have long outlived the antagonism that once arose and is now long forgotten.

The story of a single faculty member's driving pattern does, however, help focus the framework of Laurier's campus and the structure of Canadian universities as a whole. Every reader of Dr. Roy's first volume on WLU, *Recollections of Waterloo College*,[2] will be engaged by the generous focus, marked by and continued from the earliest pages. And there is something in her report of her earliest discussion of religion at

---

1 James Doyle in Jane Campbell and James Doyle, eds., *The Practical Vision: Essays in English Literature in Honour of Flora Roy* (Wilfrid Laurier University Press, 1978), pp. x–xi. Flora Roy's unpublished Ph.D. dissertation (University of Toronto, 1960) is entitled "George Berkeley and the Eighteenth Century."

2 For Dr. Roy's view of the university see her *Recollections of Waterloo College* (Wilfrid Laurier University Press, 2004) and *Recollections of Waterloo Lutheran University 1960–1973* (Wilfrid Laurier University Press, 2006).

Waterloo College that marks the later pattern of the Lutheranism that was
the focus of the early years.

> They didn't ask me [in the job interview] anything directly about reli-
> gion, but at one point in our talk I had reason to say that I didn't agree
> with Luther in everything, which seemed to amuse them. Dr. Lehman
> said: "If you could suit the sisters of St. John [where Dr. Roy, an Angli-
> can, had taught for two years while pursuing her B.A. and M.A. in
> Regina], you'll do for us."

The pattern seemed to hold for James Clark, her colleague in the English Department from the late 1940s, as well as for the regular Lutherans
of the day, including the Rev. Lloyd H. Schaus, who had graduated from
Waterloo College in 1930 and served as dean of the college from 1950 to
1967, and J. Frederick Little, chair of Philosophy, who had taught at the
university for some 30 years before his death in 1990 and who served as
a clear supporter of the Lutheran focus of the university in 1973, attempt-
ing to defend an educational agenda of the Lutheran university against
the overriding demands of most of the faculty and who challenged, for
better or for worse, changing the university's character to what it had by
that time in fact already become—one of the many schools under a
provincial charter.

The campus did indeed grow, and whether or not it will remain mind-
ful of its history is not the crucial issue. That will be decided by future
needs, whatever they might be. Crucial is that the loss of its distinctive
Lutheran foci—"Lutheran" here a stand-in for "religion" and "culture"
with an eye to that Tillichian aphorism—was emblematic of the changes
that enveloped Canada in the 1950s and 1960s and that may be revisited
in some "multicultural" manner as the future takes root.

The names of two notable professors from that earlier "Lutheran"
day—Leupold and Little—identify obscure buildings on a growing campus.[3] Dr. Roy's omission from memory on the campus may be overcome
in time (there was a brief moment when it was hoped her name would

---

3 Ulrich S. Leupold fled Nazi Germany in 1939 and remained a formidable figure on
   the campus until his death in 1970. Carol Herman Little, an American, was a noted
   professor and administrator at the Evangelical Lutheran Seminary and Waterloo
   College. He died in 1958.

be considered as important enough to be emblazoned on a central building). But (again) that is not of primary importance. For this fifty-year veteran of "WLU," reflecting on those many years, what is paramount is the focus of the institution, a focus one may hope remains that of the good Bishop Berkeley: "I imagine that thinking is the great *desideratum* of the present age: and that the real cause of whatever is amiss, may justly be reckoned the general neglect of education, in those who need it most, the people of fashion."[4]

---

4 George Berkeley, *Alciphorn, or, The Minute Philosopher. In Seven Dialigues. Containing an Apology for the Christian Religion, against those who are called Free-thinkers* (Increase Cooke [New Haven], 1803), pp. 386–87.

Chapter 25

Laurier Looks Abroad: Waterloo, Marburg, and Laurier International

ALFRED HECHT

O N DECEMBER 14, 1984, PRESIDENT JOHN WEIR OF WILFRID LAURIER University and President Walter Kröll of Philipps University in Marburg, Germany, signed a cooperative agreement for the annual exchange of four students from each university. This was Laurier's first international cooperative agreement. The exchange students would pay tuition fees for a normal course load at their home university and then take a normal course load at the host university. On their return they would be given academic credit for the courses taken abroad. Later the agreement was extended to include faculty and staff exchanges. The sending institution would pay for the travel costs to the host university and the host university would provide accommodation and some subsistence allowance.

How did Laurier come to that first agreement? For this I have to go back in time. I joined the WLU geography department in the summer of 1972 after completing my doctorate at Clark University. In 1975, when the question of tenure loomed, I thought I should look around for another job just in case. The John F. Kennedy Institute at the Free University of Berlin was advertising for an assistant professor in my field, and I applied. In the spring of 1976 I was offered the position. But by that time I had received tenure and been promoted at Laurier. Since the job in Berlin was restricted to six years, I declined it but was offered a visiting professorship for their summer semester, April to August 1976. It was my first foray into German academia.

The head of the North American geographic studies unit at the institute was Dr. Karl Lenz, a graduate of Philipps University and an expert on Canada. While in Berlin I attended a conference where Dr. Lenz introduced me to a friend of his, Alfred Pletsch of Philipps University and a budding expert on Canada. Our academic interests were well matched and we hit it off right away. In fact, by 1981 we had received a major grant of 248,000 DM ($176,030) from the Volkswagen Foundation in Germany to study "Ethnicity Problems and Aspects in Central Canada." Dr. L. Muller-Wille from McGill University in Montreal was added to the team as were a number of Canadian and German students.

We organized workshops and symposia in Canada and Germany. At an early symposium in Germany, President Kröll of Philipps asked if we would be interested in a partnership between our universities that would foster further cooperation. When this was first proposed to President John Weir at Laurier, his reaction was that he did not believe in such partnerships unless someone put some money into them, which he was unable to do. When this message was conveyed to President Walter Kröll, he answered that he knew someone who just might be willing to make such an investment. He approached Mr. Hans Viessmann, an entrepreneur who owned a major heating equipment company, Viessmann Werke GmbH & Co. KG, near Marburg, and was currently the treasurer of the Friends of the University of Marburg. Mr. Viessmann had established a small branch plant in Waterloo in 1987 and hence knew about our city. His answer was that each year his firm would provide a travel scholarship of 1,500 DM ($1,000) to the best Canadian student coming to Marburg on a student exchange. The Viessmann corporation has honoured this pledge ever since. This pledge was good enough for John Weir, and the cooperation agreement was signed. By 2005 around seventy Laurier students had studied for a semester or more at Marburg. A slightly larger number of Marburg students came to Laurier. In addition about twenty faculty and staff exchanges took place.

Mr. Viessmann's generosity to Laurier was not restricted to travel scholarships for exchange students. In 1991 he donated $13,000 to support the work of the European Faculty Interest Group at Laurier, of which I was the chair. In 1996 we held a conference in his castle in Hof, Germany, to which he contributed $9,000. During that conference, over a glass of

wine in the castle library, he announced he was setting up two endow-
ment funds at Laurier, selecting from a list of options I had given him,
one for exchange students from Laurier going to Europe ($100,000) and
one for the Geography department to upgrade software and hardware in
its computer lab ($100,000). Laurier also received $50,000 for general
campus renovations. At another meeting on January 30, 2001, again over
a glass of excellent wine, he asked me how much I wanted for further
projects. He provided 400,000 DM ($284,000 Canadian) for an endow-
ment for the establishment of a Viessmann European Research Centre at
Laurier.

After World War II Mr. Viessmann had inherited a small heating
boiler business that, by 1990, he had developed into the industry leader,
with some eight thousand employees. During this process he also acquired
over 1,300 patents. For these achievements Laurier awarded him an honorary doctorate in 1991 (Philipps University also bestowed an honorary
doctorate on him). Laurier lost a good friend and benefactor when
Dr. Viessmann died on March 30, 2002.

The signing of Laurier's first international agreement led to our participation in two Ontario-wide student-exchange agreements, one with
Rhône Alps, France, and the other with Baden-Württemberg, Germany.
During this period I administered our German exchanges and the French
department administered those in France. In the 1994–95 academic year,
under the guidance of Vice-President: Academic Rowland Smith, the
university established Laurier International (LINT), reporting directly to
the vice-president. It inherited an institution-to-institution relationship
with Marburg, the Ontario programs, a study program in Nice (run by
a number of Ontario universities), and a three-year Canada–EU multi-
centre program. The first staff person was Karen Strang and the first
director was Frank Turner, followed by Alex Murray.

In the summer of 1999, Rowland Smith appointed me director of
Laurier International and International Liaison. I received an office, a
two-course teaching release, two staff people, and the task of increasing
the international component at Laurier. According to Laurier tradition,
the budget was small and much of the travel cost had to be covered by my
research funds or by host institutions. In late 1999 Debbie King was added
to Laurier International. Her responsibilities included international recruitment (except in North America where it was the responsibility of Laurier

Liaison), responding to visa-student needs once they were at Laurier, and coordinating and giving a home to the World University Service of Canada program at Laurier.

If more Laurier students were to have an international experience, a major task was to increase the number of international partner universities. Reciprocity in student exchanges was a major requirement in cooperative agreements. Laurier would receive the provincial government grant for a student only if the Laurier student going abroad paid his/her tuition fee at Laurier while studying abroad. The incoming exchange student would then not have to pay any tuition fees at Laurier.

We were able to increase the number of Laurier partner institutions from one in 1995 to sixty-six at the start of 2005. We were also involved in a regional group (provincial or statewide) with fourteen partner universities. With this increase Laurier had about 460 student semester openings at international partner institutions to which it could send students.

The selection process for a partner institution varied but frequently involved consultation with one or more of the Laurier vice-presidents, deans, and department chairs as well as faculty, staff, and students. An agreement could be initiated by Laurier, but frequently we were responding to requests from institutions abroad. To come to an agreement required a good fit with Laurier's curriculum and language needs. Faculty interests also needed to be considered. Also important was the potential partners' academic reputation. In 2005, nineteen of our partner institutions were ranked in the top 500 universities worldwide (unfortunately, we were not). Of our partner institutions, forty-four were in Europe, 10 in the Americas, eight in Asia, two in Australia, and one in Africa.

By 2005 the number of Laurier students studying abroad had increased more then eightfold, from 14 in 1995 to 117 in 2005, a rate of increase substantially larger then the doubling of the number of full-time undergraduates over this period. That speaks well for Laurier students wanting an international experience and for LINT's ability to provide one. Laurier exchange students normally received five course credits per semester on their return.

As mentioned earlier, LINT, after 1999, also had the responsibility of coordinating international student recruitment. This too was an area of significant expansion. International undergraduate student semester enrolments increased from 224 in the 2000–01 academic years to 688 in the 2004–05 academic year. These figures include incoming exchange students at Laurier.

The university's goal was that 10% of graduating students would have an international experience. President Bob Rosehart stated, during meetings with President Lehman from the University of Applied Sciences in Hof, Germany, and with Vice-President Mr. Yoshio, from the Akita International University in Japan, that Laurier was trying to expand the international experience so that about 10% of our graduates would have some international experience even if it came from only a week or so in a formal foreign setting. As I reported to President Rosehart in 2005 at the end of my six-year term as director of LINT, this goal had been achieved.

During the 2004–05 academic year 277 Laurier students participated in international experiences: 153 studied abroad for a semester or more; an additional 124 took part in various programs abroad for a week to a month or more. This is the participation level that is expected to continue each year. Comparing annual participation numbers with the number of graduates provides an estimate of the rate of participation in international programs. In the 2004–05 academic year Laurier graduated 2,580 students. Hence the number of students with an international experience in 2004–05 as a percentage of graduates is 10.74% (277/2,580). In other words the goal of 10% was achieved by 2005.

The picture is even better when all international students at Laurier are considered. In the winter term of 2005, 331 international students were enrolled at Laurier. Of these, some 103 were exchange or short-term-study students not pursuing a degree, leaving 228 pursuing a degree. At least a quarter of these, 57, would have graduated in 2005. When added to the annual participation level of 277 we get an estimated total of 334 graduating students with an international experience. This is 12.96% of graduates, a value substantially higher than the goal of 10%. A very good overall picture!

Laurier International has carried out its mandate well, with participants enjoying the immediate benefits that come from studying abroad, whether that "abroad" is far from Waterloo for Laurier students or in Waterloo for those who have spent time at Laurier. However, as anyone who has studied abroad will testify, the effect of living and studying in another culture, often in another language, is incalculable and lasts a lifetime.

Chapter 26

The Golden Hawks Take Flight

RICH NEWBROUGH

S PORTS HAVE BEEN A PART OF THE HISTORY OF WLU AND ITS
predecessors since the 1920s, but my recollections start in the 1960s
just as we became Waterloo Lutheran. Along the way there were trials
and tribulations. I will note them, give credit to those persons instrumental in our growth and successes, and point out some of the milestones of the athletic program over the past fifty years.

I came to WLU in 1968 after serving as an officer in the United States
Marine Corps, two years of high school coaching, and four years of sales
and marketing in the United States. I found that we were considered a
small university competing with the other smaller universities and that
WLU and our athletic teams were not taken seriously by the bigger institutions. All that changed over the next five decades.

In the 1960s our athletic facilities were very limited, which had serious
effects on daily use by faculty, staff, and students as well as on the performance of our teams. The Theatre Auditorium was home base for our
athletic department but was used for many other activities as well: theatrical productions, course registrations, large classes, and final exams.
Our women's teams had no assigned dressing room; they operated out of
a very small area with only ten lockers and one showerhead. For this little
area we had three signs printed for the door as at various times it was used
for all three: Women's Dressing Room, Officials' Room, Rehab Area.

The football team was housed in the lowest part of the Theatre
Auditorium, a dark, dank dungeon with no ventilation. When pads

and uniforms got wet, they stayed wet for the whole season. The room was lit by three light bulbs and I recall only five working showerheads. In the off-season this room became our weight room, with a collection of free weights and a bench or two. On the main level we had a decent-sized dressing room for basketball and volleyball players. The gymnasium had a parquet floor, which induced shin splints. We could crowd 600 screaming fans into the gym by utilizing the stage—a scene that intimidated most of the opposing teams. Except for a lower-campus practice field, the auditorium was it.

But facilities did not deter us from some truly remarkable achievements in the sixties. The 1961 and 1962 football Hawks claimed the league championship. At the urging of Fred Nichols, David C. "Tuffy" Knight arrived in 1965 as the new director of Athletics and head basketball coach. He wasted no time in showing the athletic world that from now on WLU would be a challenger at the league and national levels. He emphasized strict discipline and a demanding work ethic that continues to this day. His basketball team won the league championship in 1965–66. Subsequent teams went on to win six league trophies in the next six years.

In 1966 Coach Knight took over the football team and led them to an undefeated season. Much to the dismay of larger universities, WLU was invited to play for the national championship in the College Bowl. The bigger schools felt insulted, but WLU was an undefeated team, as was our opponent St. Francis Xavier University, and the selection committee thought this was a perfect fit. We lost the game, but the campus came alive after this and the thirst for victories grew to be unquenchable.

In March 1968 the basketball team under Howard Lockhart, the new basketball coach, won the league and national championships. This proved to our student athletes that a small university could not only compete with larger schools but be highly successful against them.

Not to be outdone, in 1968 the football Hawks won another league championship, but this time had to win a preliminary bowl game, in Halifax against St. Mary's, before playing in the College Bowl. They defeated St. Mary's but lost to a veteran Queen's team in the College Bowl. This loss pointed out a fact of life at our university. With plenty of graduate programs, the larger schools had players in their sixth or seventh year of competition, whereas most of our players were in their first, second, or third years. It was a game of men against boys. Moreover, those graduate programs would attract transfer athletes, which gave them an additional advantage. In 1967, after our first College Bowl try, seven or eight of our players transferred to McMaster and led that team to the College Bowl. The larger universities would actually recruit our graduates, who had little trouble establishing themselves as starters at their new university.

Perhaps the biggest win of this decade was in the boardroom. A campus planning committee was meeting to set building priorities. They decided a fine-arts centre would be followed by a school of business. The president of the Student Union was a member of the committee and asked how building priorities were determined. He was told that a $5,000 donation had already been received. Legend has it that the student president then wrote out a cheque for the same amount and suggested that perhaps an athletic facility should be considered. A survey of the student body was taken and the athletic facility was the winner. Also, the football team was finally moved out of the bowels of the Theatre Auditorium into the basement of Willison Hall.

That was a great ending to a great decade in WLU athletics. Our enrolment was less than 2,500, but we had a big athletic appetite. For that College Bowl of 1968 over 2,400 advance tickets were sold on campus. The athletes of this decade are very special to our athletic tradition, for they lit the fire that now burns in the hearts of all our athletes.

Transition years: that's how to view the 1970s and 1980s. The planning phase of our new Athletic Complex was undertaken by faculty, staff, and students with great enthusiasm. Two million dollars was to be spent. In those days, you were never allowed to spend one dollar more than was budgeted. The architects advised that a full Olympic-sized pool could not be included within the budget. However, a student prepared a paper on the pros and cons of such a pool. The paper was given to President Frank Peters, who negotiated with the architects, who soon agreed that we could have an Olympic-length pool but we would have to do with six lanes rather than eight. It took only a little over a year to construct the facility and it came in $200,000 under budget! The surplus was used to construct a woodworking shop as a building annex. The area was to revert to the Department of Athletics if the shop were relocated. Somehow this proviso was forgotten and the area was seen as a possible storage facility for the library. Coach Don Smith, who never threw a piece of paper away in his life, dug into his bulging file cabinet and found the appropriate minutes of a Board of Governors meeting. The room was ours and it became our fitness centre.

As soon as we opened the new facility, a few women students complained that there was no sauna for women. They decided to use the sauna in the men's dressing area. In two days a sauna was built in the women's dressing room.

Early in this same decade all Ontario university athletics—both men's and women's—were brought under the same umbrella. A commission on university athletics was established. (The first chair was Dr. Robert Rosehart, then president of Lakehead University, who would move to WLU in 1997.) This new arrangement was the first true indication that WLU athletics was now on the same level as the rest.

In the second year of this new system, the football Hawks won the championship over Western by a 38–27 score. The championship trophy was the Yates Cup, one of the oldest team trophies in North America. The team defeated St. Mary's in the Atlantic Bowl and moved on to our third try for the national championship, only to lose to the University of Alberta. The football team would win the Yates Cup again in 1973 and 1978 but would lose out in the preliminary bowls. Our men's basketball team appeared in the national tournament twice, only to lose after a good showing.

By the end of the 1970s we were standing tall in Ontario university athletics. We also added men's soccer and later women's soccer. Both of these teams were highly competitive and were destined to bring home championships. In 1973 we became Wilfrid Laurier University, with the ceremony taking place in our new gymnasium, which could accommodate all of our students, faculty, and staff. In the last year of Waterloo Lutheran, we won the new league's football championship and in the first year of Wilfrid Laurier we won it again.

In the 1980s enrolment at WLU increased to over three thousand. A noteworthy championship was won by the women curlers in 1986; this would be a great stepping stone for the future of this sport at WLU. The men's hockey team brought home league championships in 1983 and 1989. The men's soccer team captured league championships in 1980 and 1987 while the women won a championship in 1989. In just a few short years our soccer teams had become perennial contenders for league titles and national honours. Our women's basketball team was not very successful early in this era but in the mid-eighties came to life under Coach Gary Jeffries and his assistant Fred Nichols. They not only won games, they made the playoffs! The league was so impressed they allowed us to host the basketball championship, in the process showing off our new facilities.

In the 1990s the Hawks took full flight. University enrolment increased every year, passing the five thousand mark and continuing upward. In 1991 the football Hawks won the Yates Cup with a dramatic victory over archrival Western. The team then won the Churchill Bowl over Queen's and moved on to our fourth try at the national championship, now called the Vanier Cup. We defeated Mount Allison, a momentous occasion. As soon as we arrived back on campus, the party was on! The gymnasium was overflowing with well-wishers, as were Wilf's and the Turret. There were mini-parties within the residences; it seemed as if everyone was on campus that night. It had been twenty-three years since the basketball Hawks had come home with a national title—a first for WLU. The Vanier was an important victory for WLU; it ended any notion of a football "hex" and proved that our teams of this era could compete and win at the national level.

We didn't wait long for the next title: the women's soccer team came home victorious in 1992, a feat they would repeat in 1995. In the mid-nineties a women's hockey team was established. What they have done is almost a miracle. In the next fifteen years this team would always start and finish among the nation's top-ranked teams: a dynasty was born.

In this decade we upgraded our football facilities by purchasing Seagram Stadium from the city of Waterloo for the princely sum of one dollar. We added artificial turf and were soon the envy of the league. The Athletic Complex was totally refitted and modernized with a state-of-the-art fitness center.

The decade 2000–11 turned out to be a record-setting decade of domination—and a real challenge to the athletes of the future. Our newly created women's lacrosse team won eight league titles. The women's hockey team brought home eight league titles in nine years. Our men's soccer teams won league titles in 2000, 2001, and 2008 and the national title in 2008. Women's basketball made two trips to the championship without a medal but in 2011 came home with the bronze.

Our football team won back-to-back league championships, going undefeated in league play both years, a record for WLU football. In 2004 we lost to Laval University on their home turf, but we came home with one thought: we will get better in all aspects of the program. Laval had started a football program only a few years before, but they became the closest thing to big-time university football we had seen in Canada in the last forty years. Any football game at Laval was a huge event, with all of the glitter possible. Laurier's manager of football operations and head coach, Gary Jeffries, set out to duplicate the Laval scenario as much as possible. We went undefeated again the next season and won our second national football championship. The game went to the wire as we kicked the winning field goal in the final minute of play. To reach this goal, the team won twelve games, four in post-season play, also a WLU record. In all, the Hawks won eighteen league titles and six national titles in this decade.

In 2007 the grand opening of University Stadium was held with lots of new things: turf, dressing rooms, seating, lighting, and washrooms. On the lower campus we built Alumni Field, now the home of our soccer teams. The swimming pool in the Athletic Complex needed a complete overhaul and, at the last minute, donations from government, various associations, and our students made this possible. With two playing fields with artificial surfaces, a brand new stadium, and an attractive and functional athletic complex, we are second to none. When our alumni return to campus, most stare in disbelief and astonishment when they compare our present-day facilities and programs with those of the 1960s.

The Golden Hawks have truly taken wing. Who knows how high they'll be flying over the next fifty years? It has been a privilege to have been part of this picture, first as an assistant football coach and lecturer in physical education, then as head football coach and director of Athletics and Recreation, and, most recently in retirement, supporting Golden Hawks football through fundraising and recruiting. Where else could I have experienced such excitement and enthusiasm and success by our teams?

Part Four

Quotidian: The Day-to-Day
(Or, Keeping the Wheels Turning)

Chapter 27

Getting Everyone and Everything Just Right

JIM WILGAR

I DROVE MY DAD'S 1959 STUDEBAKER WITH THREE FRIENDS FROM Barrie to Albert Street and parked in a lot marked "Reserved" at what was then Waterloo College. That was the beginning of a wonderful journey that changed not only my life but also the lives of too many to contemplate.

A "Preliminary Year" option was the goal. It had been discussed earlier with my parents. Children of some of their friends had also attended and loved "the Lutheran College" in Waterloo affiliated with the University of Western Ontario at the time.

We were invited into the board room to meet with a quiet, caring man by the name of Dr. Lloyd Schaus. His thoughtful suggestions and uncomplicated entry procedures soon had us enrolled in programs that would set us on a path of higher expectations and hopes. Exactly who did the admissions and registration and how it all happened I didn't know then. Dr. Schaus's approach was more one of genuine personal interest and helpful guidance. This student-centred focus was a hallmark of this college! Now I was a recipient of that focus and would in time carry that philosophy forward as a goal to get "everyone and everything just right."

My appreciation of our classes and the faculty in those early years in Geography (Dr. Krueger), English (Jim Clark, Dr. Roy), Economics (Dr. Max Stewart), and Psychology (Dr. Mary Kay Lane, Dr. Morgenson) was further enhanced by the enjoyable times outside of those small classes. Problems were often dealt with in the Torque Room, the Circus Room, and even at lunches in Waterloo Park or in a faculty member's home. Oh, yes, there was a new "sister" university down the street that had originated at Waterloo College, but we paid little or no attention to it except at rival sporting events.

The Canadian Officers Training Corps provided much-appreciated spending money, an officer's rank, a half-credit, and exciting summer training and employment. Many clubs and sports, the Winter Carnival, being part of the Bed Pushing Team, our successful football teams, and many other athletic achievements all enhanced what came to be known as the "The Laurier Experience."

The combination of great teachers and staff willing to assist you, along with student activities of every description, all helped set a foundation for life not just for me but for all who recognized how very fortunate we were to be at Waterloo College and then Waterloo Lutheran University. Those classes and the "experience" of WLU were helping me to focus on getting things right.

After graduating in 1964, I taught geography, physical education, English, and other subjects in Midland, Ontario, only to feel the pull of a graduate degree. After assessing the alternatives, WLU again became my preferred choice. Could I pass GMAT tests, fulfill all the requirements, and graduate? Barb (my wife-to-be), fellow WLU geographer Ken McCleary, Dean of Students Fred Nichols, and a truly devoted staff and faculty helped me to focus my goals and areas of interest. Within a few years I was awarded my M.A. in geography. Teaching part-time in the geography labs and at WLU's summer extension program in Orillia were great opportunities to hone my teaching skills and broaden my knowledge of geography and resource planning as well as of the university at large. My thesis advisor, the late Dr. George Priddle, and WLU faculty and students who became lifelong friends were inspirations in more ways than they will ever know.

But there was the matter of an outstanding bill owed to the university. Though we (Barb and I had married in the summer of 1967) were serving as the head residents of "Grad A," which blessed us with an income of a dollar per student per month, money was tight. As luck would have it, while I was standing in the Business Office line one day, Cliff Bilyea mentioned to me that Steve Little was moving to the University of Waterloo and there would be an opening in the Office of the Registrar. I applied, had various interviews, and before the ink had dried on the other job applications I had submitted, I found myself as the liaison-admissions officer of my beloved university, working for Registrar Henry Dueck and, more specifically, Keith Rae, director of Admissions. One initial task was to assist with the move of the Registrar's Office from the soon-and-sadly-to-be-demolished Willison Hall to the ground floor on the southwest corner of the newly erected Central Teaching Building.

While working many a paper route when I was growing up, I had pushed lots of "paper." But that was nothing compared to the seemingly endless mounds of files, transcripts, and letters that routinely came my way as part of the new job. Those blizzards of paper and related assessments and phone calls were interspersed with liaison trips to secondary schools throughout Ontario marketing our "Lutheran–non-Lutheran" university. Compared with what other liaison officers brought to these road shows, I thought we were high-tech, as we had a slide show, full-colour brochures, and maybe more enthusiasm and conviction than even Martin Luther himself!

What a chance to help prospective students and their parents learn about a university that, though one of the smaller in Ontario, offered a chance for a post-secondary education in life! I am ever grateful for the breadth of experience I gained in that position and the opportunities to learn about the many facets of liaison and admissions, indeed the whole administrative process. It extended well beyond those piles of papers and files.

In 1970 the University of Western Ontario hired me to be their director of Admissions. Of particular interest was the gym-sized room that housed the new mainframe IBM. In an adjoining space were a host of IBM computer card machines and operators. The Admissions Office handled the files and the thousands of punched cards of those applying to the faculties of Arts and Sciences, Engineering, Dentistry, Law, and Medicine.

The job provided an opportunity to learn the scope of the "registrar" function and to work with Western's various faculties and schools as well as with the affiliated colleges and, not least, with a host of very talented people. During this time I had the opportunity to play a part in the creation of the new Ontario Universities Application Center (OUAC) under the direction of Herb Pettipiere of the University of Guelph. Initiated by the Council of Ontario Universities, this initiative was unique in that all secondary school students now applied on a common application form through OUAC to a maximum of three choices of post-secondary degree-granting institutions in Ontario. To have served in the development of this initiative and to play a role in many provincial, national, and international admissions and registrarial organizations was again linked to the experiences and opportunities Laurier had provided. Even though my paycheque was from Western—which sometimes dominated Laurier on the gridiron—my heart was Purple and Gold!

In 1976 a Purple and Gold opportunity came my way: to return to our alma mater. To leave beautiful London, uproot family, and leave behind friends was a difficult decision. My first day at what had become Wilfrid Laurier University brought back the privilege (and fun) of working with talented, dedicated staff whom I had known earlier—Helene Forler, Janet Heimpel, Careen Andrews, Keith Rae, Jacqueline Heit, Arthur Stephen. The basis for success in any undertaking, I believe, is to fully appreciate the skills and knowledge of others around you and to draw on their ideas and strengths to supplement one's own.

Vice-President Neale Tayler had asked me to be the registrar but also to assume the role of secretary of senate "for a short time." What would that entail? To answer that question, with the dedicated help of my executive assistant Jacqueline Heit we contacted all Ontario secretaries of senate and board secretaries only to find that there wasn't an association from which to learn the trade. Laurier hosted the first meeting of a new provincial association affectionately referred to as SOUSE (Secretaries of Ontario University Senates Etc.). This body helped many serving in those positions to realize the importance of their role in university governance and policy formulation at the senate and board levels.

The processes associated with having mounds of paper and endless files that had haunted me when I set foot in the Registrar's Office still needed to be addressed. Laurier was growing! Laurier's new Xerox Sigma 7 computer had tremendous capacity but so far hadn't been directed to deal with student records. The search for someone to design and implement such a program led to our neighbour down the street.

The development team, led by Werner Ullman, produced a dramatically improved system for tracking student records. Information from initial inquiry, prior educational data, and assessment of admissibility were key changes. University program- and course-selection options, along with exam results, were improved. The new software also monitored student progression and graduation eligibility. A new kind of examination schedule, adopted by some other Ontario universities, maximized space usage, eliminated exam conflicts, and minimized sequential exams. Data for convocations, finance, and government reporting as well as alumni records were but a click away. Well, most of the time.

Growth through excellence—cogently conveyed to the wider public by Arthur Stephen's liaison work—was evident in the development of new and innovative undergraduate and graduate programs. The faculties of Music, Social Work, and Arts and Science, and the School of Business and Economics required constant expansion of faculty and physical plant. This growth included a strong professional student-service component.

Named as the first Associate Vice-President of Student Affairs, I was responsible for non-academic and non-financial sectors of the university. In this role I had the enjoyable challenge and responsibility of working closely with the heads of Athletics (Rich Newbrough), Career Services and Placement (Jan Basso), Human Resources (Earl Rayner), and the Registrar's Office (Peter Tron), as well as the Dean of Students (Fred Nichols), and their very capable staffs. There were some very memorable situations. Highlights include winning the Vanier Cup and being a part of many other Golden Hawk athletic achievements as well as labour negotiations, new telephone systems, Colpoys Bay retreats, food-service changes, new computer (Banner) and systems integration, and even the Hay System of salary rationalization. The annual cycles of admissions, registration, Frosh Week, and convocations were exhilarating. There was rightly a new focus on enhancing women's rights and women's athletics as well as on workplace safety and programs directed toward those with physical challenges. Enhanced residence-life programs and new building projects along with departmental moves, creative student-placement programming, and staff changes were but a small fraction of the issues that required many long hours of my time.

And, yes, serving as the secretary of senate continued. I also felt it important to *project* Laurier. As a dedicated member of the Kitchener

Conestoga Rotary Club and participant in many church and community fundraising events, I could offer assistance to those organizations in ways that brought to them a Laurier presence.

Over the years I had the privilege of working with four presidents: Frank Peters, Neale Tayler, John Weir, and Lorna Marsden. Looking back over more than thirty years in the service of higher education and in particular to Wilfrid Laurier University, I was very proud of what had been accomplished and how an ever-improving and innovative "Laurier Experience" had enhanced many lives. Now a new challenge presented itself. President Marsden asked me to chair an institutional downsizing committee she had struck in response to severe financial cutbacks imposed by the province. The deadline was very strict, but with the able assistance of graduate student and editorial assistant Marie Malloy, the committee, representing the various university faculties and administrative divisions, produced a report (submitted on time!) that set forth a "financial reduction model." That model, coupled again with my "Laurier Experience," was presented at provincial and national conferences as well as at Griffith University, Australia, in 1997 as part of our six-month house exchange.

Retirement from Laurier provided the opportunity for a new venture: working in wind energy development with my eldest son, Jay, and other associates. While at Laurier I had worked closely with a variety of people within the university, in provincial ministries, municipalities, and other areas. That experience has been a great asset in dealing with landowners, ministries, and municipal governments regarding our energy projects. Working with conservation authorities and consultants has taken me back to my graduate-student days in geography and resource management. It has been inspiring to do research, give lectures, and conduct tours of wind project sites with members of the public, professors, and students who know all too well the importance of moving toward production of more renewable electrical energy.

It is also very satisfying to see son Jay and his wife, Nancy, daughter Jackie, and son Andrew with Laurier parchment on their walls—some even ̣aring their dad's signature in the lower-right corner. And now grandsons are enjoying their own Laurier Experience from the nds as they watch football and soccer games while munching ̣ot dogs.

Little did I realize how my forty years of experience at Laurier would help me to try and "Get Everyone and Everything Just Right" on so many levels and in so many ways. Laurier helped me with that objective, and in turn I was (and am) glad to have helped Laurier.

Chapter 28

Five Years as University Secretary

FRANK MILLERD

I HAD FINISHED TWO TERMS AS CHAIR OF THE DEPARTMENT OF Economics and was on sabbatical at the University of Portsmouth in England in 1994 when President Lorna Marsden called and asked if I would take on the job of university secretary, then vacant, when I returned to campus. The call was a complete surprise. When I left on sabbatical leave the job was in good hands. After some thought and discussion I said I would take the job. I was a member of the search committee that had recommended that Lorna be offered the position of president and, having had some role in her coming to WLU, felt an obligation to help out. It was not to be a full-time job; I would be able to continue with some teaching and research.

When I started, many asked me what the university secretary did. That was a good question; it was a relatively new position on campus. Most Canadian universities had such a position; in some Quebec universities the position is impressively called the "Secretary-General." Many of the duties had previously been spread around campus. For example, the Board of Governors was supported by the President's Office, the Senate by the Registrar's Office. Many of these functions needed to be brought together to improve the efficiency and effectiveness of our governing bodies, an aspect of the maturing of the university. There was also a need to respond better to external requests and obligations: briefs to government commissions had to be prepared; legislative and regulatory compliance reports had to be presented. Many of the responsibilities of the job were mandated, but there was some opportunity to innovate both in carrying out the required duties and in developing new areas.

A major responsibility of the office was setting dates, planning, preparing agendas, gathering and distributing supporting documentation, taking minutes, and following up on actions and issues for a constant and almost endless series of meetings. There was the Board of Governors, the Senate, their executives and committees, board retreats, ad hoc committees, a planning committee, a presidential search committee, and various meetings of administrators. Since some of the topics were common to several groups, you sometimes wondered which meeting you were in. With our bicameral system it was important that the Senate and the board were informed of each others' activities, which meant another series of reports.

Producing the minutes of a meeting could be a challenge. Senate meetings were tape recorded, but I was not prepared to sit through the meeting again. No speaker, except if their title or role was relevant, was ever identified in the minutes. But providing a fair discussion of the arguments presented could be difficult, and, a couple of times, corrections were requested. As my typing improved I used a laptop to take minutes, having previously loaded the agenda and preset motions into the computer. After editing what I had entered during the meeting, a decent set of minutes could be prepared. An occasional problem was maintaining a quorum as a meeting continued. A few times I had to ask a participant to return to a meeting so a crucial vote could be taken.

The external board members generously donated their time and talent to the university but were not always aware of academic activities. We instituted a board breakfast where outstanding students could meet board members. The board also heard from the vice-presidents and deans about activities in their areas.

One accomplishment was setting up an institutional research office. Previously, when the university was called upon to submit a report to one of the many government commissions, the relevant statistics were not always readily available. Various offices of the university collected and published information but in varying formats and for varying time periods. The lack of a centralized source of consistent information hindered effective planning, delayed our responses to requests for information, and limited the current awareness by faculty and staff of the university's activities. This problem was highlighted when, in an early meeting, a participant suggested that the university grow to 6,000 full-time under-graduate students. On returning to my office later that day I found we were already at 6,300 full-time undergraduates.

To start an institutional research office we received a budget to hire a student for the summer. Thus prepared, I interviewed business and economics co-op students for two days, believing that, with their train-ing in analytical methods, one would be ideally suited for this summer job. I thought the job was appealing; the work would be interesting and challenging and, of course, the boss was excellent. I carefully ranked those I interviewed and awaited the successful applicant. But all those interviewed wanted to work in corporate Canada; not one picked our job in their ranking. So, I went back to Career Services for another round of interviewing. I managed to convince Jodie MacIntosh, an honours Biology student, to work in our office for the summer and she did an excellent job. Wally Pirker then took on the responsibility for institutional research and today produces an excellent annual institu-tional data and statistics book, covering enrollment, students, faculty and staff, physical resources, space allocation, finances, the library, alumni, and research.

The secretariat was also responsible for developing and maintaining the university's policies and procedures (it is now available on the WLU website). This entailed drafting policies, obtaining comment on poli-cies, identifying areas where policy revision or development was needed, getting the policies approved, and communicating policies to the univer-sity community. Often this required some research. How, for example, should academic misconduct be defined? When should university flags be flown at half-mast? I found my experience as a faculty member was of some benefit in drafting policies as well as in other areas.

One of the duties of the position was assisting with the planning of convocation and other university ceremonies. For convocation this usu-ally involved some form of coordination, as the various responsibilities for convocation were spread around campus. Some volunteers were con-cerned about the ceremonial side of convocation. I assured them that, since most of those attending had never been to a convocation ceremony, as long as the proceedings were suitably dignified and organized the cer-emony would be fine.

A dinner for the honorary-degree recipients preceded each convocation. The secretariat was asked to arrange the dinner. Booking the room and sending out invitations was simple, but what about the menu, the table arrangements, and other such details? This was well beyond my capabilities and interest, so we were very fortunate to be able to hire someone, often a faculty spouse, to look after those aspects of the dinner.

One of the ceremonies the secretariat coordinated was the opening of the new science building. How to make this a suitably impressive ceremony? In the first few meetings of those involved in organizing the ceremony, various impressive and complex plans were put forward. But, one weekend, as I was watching the start of the hockey season with my sons, we saw the Vancouver Canucks, who had won their conference the season before, hoisting a commemorative banner in their rink. A nice ceremony, but the banner was going up crooked, one side higher than the other. If a professional hockey team with a large budget could not do such a ceremony correctly, what hope did we have? Thus, the opening of the new building was kept as simple as possible and, in the end, I believe, was suitably impressive.

Another issue was finding a prefix for the rooms in the new science building. You may wonder how we settled on "N." We couldn't use "S," as that was reserved for the seminary building. At the time of opening, the science building was the *N*ewest building, so "N" it was.

One of the responsibilities of the job was attending the annual meeting of Canadian university board chairs and secretaries. The board members were an impressive bunch; I have never seen so many holders of the Order of Canada in the same room. In some cases the board secretary was a member of the board, supported by a secretariat, such as at WLU; in other cases the board secretary was the university secretary or equivalent.

Board secretaries met to discuss various administrative matters. One concern of many was how to find out how other universities handled an issue or problem when this issue or problem arose on their campus. There was no efficient way to do this; this was the 1990s, before widespread use of the internet. The solution was an internet discussion group that we set up and hosted at WLU, open to university secretaries or the equivalent. When dealing with an issue or providing advice to someone on

campus, university secretaries could quickly canvass most of their coun-
terparts across Canada about administrative and procedural matters,
thereby gathering useful background information for the situation at
their own institution. A sampling of the subjects of inquiries included
mandates of fundraising committees, presidential search procedures,
policies on naming buildings, procedures for dismissing students, ethical investments, and the composition of governing boards. Over fifty
such inquiries were usually made each year. The answers helped shape
policies at the inquiring institutions. It meant that universities did not
have to decide on an issue in isolation and that some consistency was
established across universities.

While university secretary I was blessed with an excellent administrative assistant: Whitney Densmore. Extremely well organized, a whiz
with word processing, always there when needed, and calm when dealing with deadlines, Whitney kept the secretariat functioning smoothly
and effectively.

After one term of five years I gave up the position and returned to
being a full-time faculty member. I was asked if I missed being at the
"centre of the action." At first I did miss participating in the various groups
and wondered how certain matters were being dealt with. After a while,
however, I didn't even know what issues were on the table, and full-time
teaching and research certainly more than made up for those many and
various administrative activities I had engaged in for five years.

Chapter 29

On Students and Deaning

FRED NICHOLS

*O*N THE FALL OF 1963 MARLENE AND I ARRIVED ON CAMPUS WITH our family of three young boys aged one, three, and five. We rented a house on Bricker Street owned by the university. Our home soon became the place to be for various students, on Wednesday nights for just talk and on Saturday nights for *Hockey Night in Canada*—so long as we had a TV set and a few cold 50s in the fridge.

The university was a lot different then. Students numbered about a thousand. Tuition, a room in residence, and a six-day meal plan came to $1,040 a year. Where the Athletic Complex is now located you would have found Swan's Cleaners and Wolfe's Farm. A cider mill stood where Alumni Field is now situated. What was the football field back then soon became the site of the president's house, now Alumni Hall.

When Dr. Villaume hired me, I remember him saying, "You will be a resource and a friend of the students." I took that to heart and from that day until June of 1997, when I retired, my loyalty was to the students and student leaders. If there was to be mutual trust and respect, I did not want to be privy to anything the administration did not want the students to know. I promised myself not to keep any secrets from the student leaders with whom I shared office space.

During the sixties, there were a few wannabe radicals—both students and faculty. It was the time of protests and we were no different in this respect from other campuses throughout North America. Some of our young professors had a way of stirring up the students. However, I believe our students worked in more co-operative ways to earn parity with the university administration in decision-making.

In Waterloo Lutheran's early years we were a dry campus, but that didn't stop our students from an occasional case of over-consumption and run-in with the law—and an opportunity to challenge my authority. Those were the times I remember the most, as they gave me a reason to build on the mutual respect I was always working to establish with the students. I had developed a close relationship with the City of Waterloo police before they were amalgamated into the Region of Waterloo force, and our students soon realized this.

I especially remember one night, during exams, when a power outage in Waterloo created a blackout on campus. Alas, a chance for the men in residence to break into the women's residence and "liberate" it from the very strict rules on visiting privileges. Under those rules the women students had to sign in and out, and if one of them had a male guest on a Sunday afternoon (the only time that was allowed), she had to leave the door to her room open. A full-time paid staff member who served as the house mother in Clara Conrad Hall, the women's residence, saw to it that the rules were observed.

I had always told our security staff that I did not want to be called at home unless things got out of hand. Well, on that night it seems that the police were called, and our security staff and the police together could not control the crowds. So I got the call. I arrived, not really knowing what to do. What I did do was to grab a flashlight from a security officer and begin wandering through the crowd. Occasionally, I would hear, "Uh-oh, it's the dean." In three instances, I tapped a student on the shoulder and said, "Come to my office tomorrow morning," and then moved on to where the crowd had gathered in the quadrangle of Clara Conrad Hall. Once they saw me, all got quiet and the serenading stopped. I said, "Okay, fun's over, now get the hell out of here." They all took off, scooting back to their residence. The next day, those three students showed up at my office, and I told them the same thing I had said the night before—"Get the hell out of here"—and they left my office smiling. Later, when the residence dons told me the students had been asking, "Who is he to make us run away like that?" I knew that the mutual respect was working.

During the 1960s and 1970s some of the students were engaging in food fights in the dining hall, upstaging the 1978 movie *Animal House,* as it were, until they themselves realized the fights were not such a good idea and quietly abandoned them. And there were the infamous panty raids that began as a fun activity in the early years but got out of hand and were banned in 1989. Initiations in campus clubs and on athletic teams also came under a ban.

In 1961, student leaders at WLU were looking for a way to have fun and yet provide for a charity during Orientation Week. Paul Enns, president of the sophomore class that year, suggested shining shoes in exchange for donations; over $1,300 was raised, and Shinerama (on which WLU holds a copyright) was born. In those very early years of Shinerama, people would submit requests for which charity to support each year. Then, in 1964, cystic fibrosis was chosen as the charity for Shinerama. The Cystic Fibrosis Canada website notes that "Shinerama is now Canada's largest post-secondary school fundraiser," with more than sixty-five universities and colleges participating and generating nearly $22 million since 1964. Remember: it all started with students at WLU.

During the early years at WLU another significant event was Winter Carnival. My office was in the downstairs area of the Campus Centre, the former Student Union Building, along with the Winter Carnival staff, who worked year-round. Our carnival received national recognition in newspapers and magazines, competing for attention with the Winter Carnival in Quebec City. On every Canadian campus, there were contests held to select a campus queen. In January of each year, Air Canada flew all the university queens to WLU for the week-long festivities. Each was provided with an escort during her stay. The "Miss Canadian Snow Queen" (on which WLU held a copyright) was crowned during the carnival. There was a big parade, ice sculptures were built, and celebrity judges came to campus. One year, Nancy Greene, the Olympic skier, was one of these. Another time game-show host Alex Trebek served as master of ceremonies. Many well-known artists performed at the Kitchener Auditorium during the carnival, including Diana Ross and the Supremes, Stevie Wonder, the Four Preps, and Gordon Lightfoot.

The Campus Centre was very important. In those early years it was in the building where Health Services is now located. It dated back to 1960. Enrolments grew, however, and in 1965–66 student fees were increased so that we could eventually build a bigger, better campus centre. It opened its doors in 1973. The top two floors were completed first, with parking available underneath. We assumed from the start that we would eventually build the bottom two floors as well; that happened in 1995, giving us the present four-storey structure. In 1997 it was renamed the Fred Nichols Campus Centre.

In 1969 the students and the dean's office created a Dean's Advisory Council, a group of elected students who would work with me on matters pertaining to student life. We met weekly to deal with issues of conduct and other concerns that had come up during the past seven days. Establishing discipline was an integral part of the work of the council. That was in fact the number-one reason for creating the council: students tended to do a better job of dealing with discipline and issues than I could—they were very strict. I did not have a vote; unless there was a tie, the students made the decisions. The consequences of infractions could include being banned from social activities, the pubs, and campus events, or being placed on probation. A student placed on probation seldom got into trouble again.

I remember one particular case quite well. In 1987 it was reported to us that a student had stolen a jacket from the bookstore. The council's decision was to require the student to work at the bookstore for twenty-five cents an hour until he had worked enough hours to equal three times the cost of the jacket that he had stolen. The bookstore initially said, "You are punishing *us*," but the council explained that we preferred to "create ways to encourage honesty." In time, the student and the bookstore staff became friends.

In the early 1970s we created an Operating Procedures Agreement (OPA). The OPA was between the student government and the university. It stated that the students would not compete with food services or the bookstore, provided the university would not compete with the students' sale of alcoholic beverages. Because of the OPA, the student union policed the liquor licence and it entrusted the students with more responsibility. The students would not allow anything to jeopardize that liquor licence. We were always aware of potential problems and tried to educate the students before these became a big issue.

I worked very hard to get the trust of students so that we could deal with important things when a need arose. Drugs were never a big problem at WLU because we never allowed it to become a problem on our campus. We worked closely with the students, residence dons, the local police, and the RCMP. Drugs tended to be more of a problem in high schools than in universities.

I maintained a discretionary fund to assist students who might be confronted with an unexpected emergency. I give credit to a special group of alums who would contact me every year to make sure we had money available in the fund. If a student needed to get home because of a personal problem and didn't have the money, the student leaders on campus would send the person to me. My secretary and I were the co-signers of the cheques written on the discretionary fund account. It was a life-saver for many students.

My time at Laurier has been so memorable. Even so, at times it can be difficult to remember some of the things that happened during the forty-eight years I have been associated with WLU. These days I assist the Development Office in fundraising for the university. As I sit in my office in Alumni Hall, I can see my name on the Campus Centre Building just a few steps away. Imagine having your name on a popular building on a university campus and being able to look out your window to see it displayed before you. And to have been awarded an honorary degree in 2008 makes me even more proud to have been a part of the growing up of WLU.

When I think I have said it all, still more memories come to mind, but that will have to be for another chapter and another day.

Chapter 30

A Picture Is Worth a Thousand Words—AV and Beyond

WILHELM E. ("WILLI") NASSAU

To JUSTIFY THE TITLE OF THIS ESSAY, IT SHOULD REALLY BE composed of images—but perhaps around "a thousand words" might be permitted.

How did I get together with good old WLU? More basically, how did I get to Canada from Vienna? After finishing high school in Vienna, I studied fine arts and photography at the State Academy of Fine Arts in Vienna. I worked in various jobs, especially learning the new technology of colour photography, but occasional assignments also allowed me to learn cinematography at film studios in Vienna as well as in Berlin. This led to doing location research and background photography in the shooting of the noir film *The Third Man* (1949), starring Joseph Cotten, Trevor Howard, Alida Valli, and Orson Welles, which won the Oscar for cinematography that year.

Television started in Austria after a long period of experimentation in a lab that had operated clandestinely, since the Russian occupation forces would not permit television. In order to get a job at the state-owned television station, I had to take some courses in electronic engineering. I received a diploma from the Technological Trade Museum in Vienna and started eagerly to shoot 16mm films for television. During the ski championship at Schladming, Austria I met the not-yet-famous Eric Duerschmied, who was shooting for the CBC. He hired me to work on a documentary on Yugoslavia, then under Communist rule. The documentary, broadcast in Canada, resulted in an invitation to Ottawa to work for the CBC.

On November 15, 1959, I arrived in Ottawa with my own equipment, which included a new experimental transistorized audio system. One of my first assignments was an interview with Prime Minister John Diefenbaker, who allowed me quite some time and took some personal interest in my professional work. After some work for the CBC and assignments for the National Film Board, I met Ernest Bushnell, who with Stuart Griffiths started CJOH, the first private television station in Ottawa.

Because of my special interest in technical innovations I left the CBC to work on a variety of projects. Videotape was gradually replacing film. However, for a while I kept working with film. I went to Cyprus during the political crisis to shoot with Larry Henderson for the new CTV network. I also had the opportunity to shoot a colour documentary in Cyprus. Taking on freelance assignments allowed for a variety of exciting opportunities and adventures. I was always trying something new and different.

During Expo 67 I was working on assignment for the CBC at Montreal and had the opportunity to meet with visiting VIPs. One sunny day a group of people that included the president of the Lutheran Church in America and some professors were our guests. During a very pleasant lunch they talked about a small but ambitious institution named Waterloo Lutheran University. I knew nothing about Waterloo and even less about that university. Dr. Herman Overgaard mentioned some progressive ideas about teaching, and I was allowed to give my opinion about television and film not only as a subject for teaching but also as a medium in teaching.

Soon after this I went to work for a TV station in Vermont, where I had the opportunity to work on various projects at the University of Vermont at Burlington and to see some practical application of just such possibilities. I observed the operation of a modern audio-visual department and formed some more of my own ideas. Quite a bit later, I received a phone call from another progressively minded faculty member from WLU, Dr. Flora Roy. As a result I had the opportunity to come to WLU on a blustery winter day and give a brief presentation in a small lecture hall, room 2c8, in the Arts Building.

Some friendly conversation followed and soon my wife, Hermine, and I were driving to Waterloo to look for a place to live. With us, as always, was our faithful Dachshund Maxi. For a night we were invited to occupy WLU's rather lavish guest quarters. Maxi was probably the first (and last?) canine occupant of the guest suite. Things progressed fast and on June 15, 1969, I moved into my first office at the university. It was a small room in the basement of the house on Albert Street where the English department, Dr. Roy at the helm, was located. I was about six feet from the noisy furnace and access was via a very rickety spiral set of metal stairs. For a while nobody seemed to notice me, but the few visitors I eventually enjoyed were always announced by a loud rattle of the stairs. The audiovisual equipment of the university consisted of one old 16mm projector, carefully guarded by the seminary. When one operated it—after receiving permission—it rattled as loudly as my stairs.

Soon we could move into a brand-new five-storey structure—the Central Teaching Building—where I had a proper office very near to that of Dr. Roy, who took some interest in this new venture of teaching film. Our first course was English 39, History of Film. As we progressed further, we had a program of several hands-on courses in photography, radio, and film, and even, after a while, television production. I was joined by John Durst, who became a faithful friend and companion on many trips and projects over many more years. We started Telecollege; it was not the very first to use television as a teaching tool, but, as I recall, it was the first using full colour and various other modern technical features. Some daring faculty members acted in front of our cameras and university staff members dramatized some of our case studies. Eventually, under the leadership of Werner Lindschinger, Telecollege moved into its own facilities.

John Durst and I had the joy of travelling overseas to produce various documentaries. The university generously allowed me to engage in some museum work in connection with my studies of ancient glass. We produced video programs for the new dinosaur museum at Drumheller, the newly emerging Seagram Museum, and other such projects. We also acquired some antique cameras and audiovisual equipment, forming a collection that eventually became part of the collections of the Canada Science and Technology Museum in Ottawa.

President John Weir shared my interests and because of his friendly relationship with the department we were allowed to engage in experiments like using video episodes as teaching tools in the language lab.

Visiting the University of Marburg and the Champagne vineyards of France was certainly no hardship in our professional work. We placed our cameras into ancient tombs in Egypt and aimed them at the glass furnaces of Venice and Murano.

The unavoidable retirement has not caused a large change in my lifestyle. I still work, as a volunteer, at the Canadian Clay and Glass Gallery and other museums. Gladly I occasionally return to the classroom as an instructor for the Laurier Association for Lifelong Learning.

Looking back at all those colourful years, I am grateful that I was allowed to do professionally what I liked most to do: *to capture life and beauty in pictures.*

Part Five

I Came to WLU (Where's *That?*)

Chapter 31

How I Almost Got a Job at a New University Down the Street and Instead Found a Career at WLU

LOREN CALDER

O N SEPTEMBER 1956 I PASSED THE ORAL EXAMINATION FOR MY
M.A. in Slavonic Studies at the University of British Columbia. My
subject was the political thought of Maxim Gorki, the brilliant Russian
novelist and revolutionary political activist. I was now determined to
pursue a career in teaching, research, and writing about the history and
political life of Russia and the Soviet Union. I set out to begin further studies at the University of London with the support and encouragement of
two individuals in particular. Dr. Cyril Bryner was a Russian-born, Amer-
ican-trained historian. Dr. William J. Rose, before becoming the professor of Central European History at UBC, was the past director of the
School of Slavonic and East European Studies at the University of London. A Canadian-born and -trained Rhodes scholar, he was a specialist
in Polish and Central European history.

I was thrilled at the prospect of studying at such a prestigious university in one of the world's most famous cities. My wife, Eileen, and I travelled to London by bus and boat (only the wealthy travelled by plane in
those days). While we were at sea we learned that the Suez crisis had
erupted and on our first day in London we went to Trafalgar Square to
participate in a protest demonstration where Aneurin Bevan, a brilliant
Labour Party speaker and minister in the postwar period, addressed the
gathering. With thousands of others we marched to 10 Downing Street
as the crowd shouted, "Eden must go!" London was exciting and fascinating from the very start!

My studies started with intensive language training in Russian, challenging and interesting in itself but very special and eye-opening because I was part of a small class of officers who were being trained to be military attachés, the Cold War then dominating the news. Several of the officers had flown Hurricanes and Spitfires in the Battle of Britain. Another, all of twenty-five years of age, was a submarine commander. Soon, however, I was engaged in seminars and spending hours in the library of the British Museum, where one could find every book and journal published in Russia during the nineteenth and twentieth centuries. By late 1959 I had completed the residency requirements for my degree and had my dissertation topic approved: the political thought of Iu. F. Samarin, who was a conservative nineteenth-century slavophile with reformist economic and political ideas. I had spent hours and hours working on the project. We had a two-year-old son and another child to be born within two months. It was time to come home—time to seek a university teaching position.

In accord with general practice I developed a resumé and sent it to the major Canadian universities. In early March of 1960, as I recall, I received an offer from Dr. Geoffrey Adams, chair of the Department of History of Waterloo College and Associate Faculties, to join the History department of the new University of Waterloo. Apparently a University of Toronto professor had passed my name and resumé on to him. I was given to understand that the arts faculty of Waterloo College was to become the arts faculty of the new university. My wife and I were thrilled. I had a job offer from a new Ontario university teaching courses in Russian history—it was a dream come true. Written commitments were entered into and my wife and I began packing and making arrangements to leave London. All the while I tried to make the most of what was left of my time, working in the Reading Room of the British Museum and saying goodbye to Professor Richard Hare, my thesis advisor, to Dr. Bolsover, director of the School of Slavonic and East European Studies, and to my student friends from the program and the Reading Room of the museum.

We were scheduled to leave London for Canada by boat on June 3, 1960. On May 28 I received a letter from Dr. Adams informing me that the Lutheran synod had voted not to take Waterloo College into the new University of Waterloo. He also told me that he and his colleague

Dr. Donald Savage had resigned. My job was gone. The one hope, Dr. Adams advised, was that Dean Schaus might be able to offer me a job at the college. I should proceed to Waterloo as soon as I reached Canada and see Dean Schaus. Fortunately, Dean Schaus offered me a lectureship teaching courses in Russian, British, and modern European history. So I had been hired at the University of Waterloo and ended up being offered the chance of a career at what had just become Waterloo Lutheran University.

My academic career at WLU began in September 1960. Lutheran was a small university. A number of the faculty had graduated from the college and were Lutherans. There was a chapel in the new Arts Building, but Lutheranism was not a big issue and the administration and everyone else was focused on students and good teaching. The operative administrative principle was "collegiality." There was a faculty association concerned with conditions of employment—salaries, contracts, tenure, and the like. The faculty numbered between forty and fifty and the student body between five and six hundred. There were two major academic buildings and two large houses used as residences and offices. The Arts Building was new. The other major building was Willison Hall, where the library was housed. I was given an office on the ground floor of the Arts building which I shared with Dr. Bruce Honeyford, a senior scholar who had come from the University of Toronto to teach English literature.

The history department was small too. The chairman was a brilliant young American scholar, Dr. John Warwick Montgomery, who was a passionate Lutheran theologian as well as a historian with a highly developed theory of history, set out in his book *The Shape of History*, which he promulgated in the first-year history course. George Durst was the second member of the department. I was the third, a novice with a specialization in Russian and Soviet history. However, the department taught a considerable range of courses that drew on the expertise of others at WLU. For instance, Dr. Margaret Evans, the librarian, taught British constitutional history, and Welf Heick, a Waterloo College graduate working on his Ph.D. dissertation for Duke University, helped out prior to joining the department to teach Canadian, American, and Commonwealth history.

My first year was very challenging but also very interesting. My students, and there were lots of them, were tolerant and long-suffering.

Herb Epp, one of the students to take my first Russian history course, rose to political prominence, first as Waterloo's mayor and then as a Liberal MPP. Another of my students from this period was Paul Heinbecker, who went on to a distinguished diplomatic career as an ambassador, and then as formal advisor to Prime Minister Mulroney and informal advisor to Prime Ministers Trudeau, Chrétien, and Martin, and finally as Canadian ambassador to the UN. At Lutheran he was an honours History student and quarterback of the football team. In that first year I was required to teach in the extension program as well; so I found myself in Galt doing a course on British history.

That same academic year saw Waterloo Lutheran's first convocation. Held in the auditorium of the Mutual Life Insurance building on King Street, it was an august affair with eighty-three students graduating and the convocation address delivered by George Hees, a prominent Conservative politician. It was a landmark event in the rise of Waterloo College to university status. In the next year, 1962, 113 students graduated and were treated to a convocation address by the inimitable Joey Smallwood.

Each succeeding year saw the student population grow, with corresponding increases in the faculty and the physical plant. Financial survival was a constant concern as the university was operating without provincial support. The change from Waterloo Lutheran to Wilfrid Laurier led to a larger history department and to changes in my role in the department. Welf Heick, now with his Ph.D., joined the department in 1961. Soon after, Montgomery returned to the US and Dr. Charles Paape, a new member of the department and a specialist in historical methodology, became the chair. David Leitch, a tobacco farmer, businessman, and history buff, took over the British history assignment, giving me the opportunity to develop a new course on the Soviet Union. In 1966 Dr. Jacques Goutor, a young French scholar educated in the US, joined the department to teach French history with special emphasis on the French Revolution. About the same time Dr. Peter Stinglin from Switzerland joined us to teach contemporary European history as did Dr. Arlene Miller-Guinsberg, a medievalist with a special interest in witchcraft. In 1968 Walter Shelton, who was just completing his Ph.D. at the University of British Columbia, arrived and took over our British history program. From this time on I was fully specialized in the areas that interested me most: Russia, the Soviet Union, and modern diplomatic history.

In the meantime the department had been changing in other ways. It mandated that all honours students had to write a research thesis to graduate, it developed an outreach program to bring high school teachers into its ambit by organizing annual history teachers conferences on campus, and it instituted an M.A. program. It also created an apprenticeship or summer work-term option for honours students. As retirements and professional transfers took place, the department was able to re-staff itself by hiring very interesting new faculty members. In 1969 Dr. James Harkins became our French specialist. In 1973 Prof. Richard Fuke took over the American history courses and a year or two later Prof. Terry Copp became our specialist on French Canada. Soon after arriving he developed a very popular course on warfare. Dr. Douglas Lorimer and Dr. Joyce Lorimer became our British history professors and Dr. Barry Gough, with specializations in sea power and Canadian studies, joined our Canadian contingent. In 1987, Dr. George Urbaniak, whose field was international relations, and Dr. Suzanne Zeller, a specialist in the history of science, joined the department as did Dr. Cynthia Comacchio, a specialist in women's and children's studies.

By 1967 I realized I would never finish my dissertation if I continued to teach extension courses every fall, winter, and summer, so I withdrew from the program. I finished the dissertation and was awarded the M.Phil. degree from the University of London in 1980. It was published as part of a collection of outstanding theses at the major English-language universities over a fifteen-year period. In 1976 my first book, a collaborative effort with Helen Swediuk-Cheyne and Terence Scully, was published by WLU Press. It dealt with an aspect of my dissertation research on Yuri Samarin. In 1991 I was elected president of the Canadian Association of Slavists.

A career that looked like it would begin at the University of Waterloo but commenced instead at Waterloo Lutheran University and then continued on at Wilfrid Laurier University concluded when I retired in 1994 with the rank of full professor. The rapid growth of Laurier was absorbing and challenging. I participated in every phase of the History department's development, directing honours and M.A. theses, organizing history teachers conferences, directing work-term training sessions and placements, and sitting on the departmental council, where decisions were always made on a consensual basis. It gave me special satisfaction that Dr. Leonard Friesen, a most accomplished Russian history scholar, was named to succeed me.

I am very grateful to WLU for giving me the opportunity to achieve in some measure those career ambitions of my youth. I enjoyed working with my students and colleagues and am proud to have participated in the building of a fine university.

Chapter 32

One Job + One Job + One Job = A Job

HAROLD REMUS

*N*INETEEN-SEVENTY-FOUR. US INVOLVEMENT IN THE VIETNAM War had ended and with that also the protests and teach-ins in which I had taken some part. There had been some kind of break-in at a place called Watergate in Washington, D.C., leading to high drama in the capital and the media. At home I was still using pencil and paper and my high school slide rule to track expenses because those new TI calculators remained beyond a grad student's reach. I had passed my prelims at the University of Pennsylvania across the field of religious studies and my comprehensives in my specialty, Christian Origins. In between those two tests of my character and stamina I had taken time off to work with my department chair, Claude Welch, as research associate on *A Study of Graduate Education in Religion: A Critical Appraisal* (1971), to which I contributed two chapters. The research for one of these had involved interviews of doctoral students in religious studies at assorted institutions ranging from the Ivy League to southeastern US universities and theological schools to the University of Chicago. It also had meant running punch cards with data from two thousand doctoral students through a card sorter at the Penn computing centre and then turning these into printouts for analysis of the selected variables (every time I showed up there I couldn't help thinking of ENIAC, which came into being at Penn). Good preparation for what lay ahead.

Claude had a section in the book titled *1984*, the year in which he had calculated there would be no more jobs in religious studies. But it was only

1974, I was 200-some pages into my dissertation, with no job, a mortgage, two young children, and a wife whose job as an early childhood education teacher hardly paid the bills. Maybe I should forget about academic life and migrate from my current location—Princeton, NJ—to my wife's central-Illinois home territory and look for a job as a checkout clerk in the twenty-four-hour IGA near where she had grown up. I believed, and still believe, that even if I had never found an academic position, those years as a Fulbright student in Göttingen and as a Ph.D. student at Penn would have been worth the effort and not a little struggle. Nonetheless, I wasn't quite ready to give up on the academy.

Preparing resumés and letters of application B.C. (Before Computers) was no simple matter. A Canadian department chair to whom I sent one that I had managed to type to perfection replied that my qualifications exceeded his own, but he could offer me no job. I actually got two interviews, one at a seminary in the San Francisco Bay area and another at the state university in Wichita, which offered me a job after I had accepted one that had been cobbled together for me by three individuals—Wagner, Granskou, and Glebe—at an obscure Lutheran post-secondary institution in Waterloo, Ontario, Canada.

While working as a book editor at a publishing house in Philadelphia I had served as the house editor of a book translation by some guy named Norman Wagner at that university in Canada. Then, in 1970, at the annual meeting of the Society of Biblical Literature in New York, I met him in person, along with another professor named Ulrich Leupold from the same place. Norman would soon become graduate dean at the university, alongside serving as director of the newly born Wilfrid Laurier University Press and executive director of the Council on the Study of Religion (CSR), a federation of professional societies in religious studies across North America. He needed help around the office.

David Granskou was chairing Religion and Culture at WLU, was in the same field as I, and welcomed help in teaching. I had got to know Dave through business correspondence while I was working as a translator and editor in Geneva, Switzerland, and he was employed in New York City commuting from Princeton. On moving to Princeton along with my wife, Carolyn, and our infant daughter, Elise, to serve in the Lutheran church there, I met him in person.

Delton Glebe I knew not at all, but after getting acquainted with me on my visit to the campus he was ready to accept me as an adjunct instructor in Waterloo Lutheran Seminary.

Three positions, three sources of income: I had a job—after passing Dean Gerry Vallillee's litmus test of intelligent discussion of some ancient classical Greek texts with him.

It was a classic case of old boys' club—or to put a fancier name to it, "networking," a term I picked up from one of the first two books published by Wilfrid Laurier University Press: Grace Anderson's *Networks of Contact*, a study of the role of networking in finding jobs in the Portuguese community in Toronto.

As a teaching assistant and through teaching a couple of courses on my own at the University of Pennsylvania, I had acquired some teaching experience and at Laurier settled into that routine, meaning that I was commonly one session ahead of the class. In the office of the CSR in Centre Hall (now Alumni Hall and once the president's house), what did I do? Rather, what did I not do?

For the first two years I helped organize the annual meetings of the two largest professional societies in religious studies. They met at fancy hotels in Washington, D.C., and Chicago, chosen as venues because they could accommodate several thousand scholars and had a hall big enough for all the book publishers who showed up to exhibit their wares and to make contact with potential authors.

I served as managing editor of the *Bulletin*, the Council's newsletter published five times a year. I oversaw the production of *TOIL—Teaching Opportunities Information Listing*—Norman's ingenious low-cost publication with the whimsical cover that also appeared five times a year. And right away I was charged with being the founding managing editor of what was to become the omnibus book-reviewing journal in religious studies in North America, *Religious Studies Review*. The *Bulletin* expired a couple of years ago along with the CSR, as did *TOIL* many years prior. *Religious Studies Review*, now published by Wiley-Blackwell, continues our policy of long review articles and something like a thousand small review notes over the annual course of four issues. For a couple of years I was also the managing editor of *Studies in Religion/Sciences Religieuses*, the omnibus journal in religious studies in Canada. It was one of a number of journals which, plagued by prohibitive printing costs, found that the CSR or the Press assured them quality along with reasonable costs and tender loving care.

In between classes and trying to finish my dissertation, I was involved in various ways in Wilfrid Laurier University Press, which was also located in Centre Hall.

I say "I." That is shorthand. The staff of the CSR and the Press made it all possible, aided and abetted by Hart Bezner, director of Computing Services, and his staff, who made possible the very complicated operations of the CSR generally and of *Religious Studies Review* in particular. Doreen Armbruster's chapter in this book gives details of how the Press evolved into one of the leading university presses in Canada. Before "Laurier" had become a household word in Canadian academia, the booth where I stood and displayed WLU Press titles at the annual meetings of the Learned Societies helped put the new university on the map.

Ladona Riegert for many years tracked the accounts of both the CSR and the Press, ever there with her trusty calculator to figure out costs of publishing books and to record the dues paid by the CSR member societies, which Cathy Wagner, until her departure, recorded on punch cards that she carried over to the computer in the Central Teaching Building to be turned into printouts that were mailed to the executives of the CSR's constituent societies. Heather Blain and Mary Wagner cut and pasted both the CSR and WLU Press publications into being. On the database that Hart and staff had set up, Helen Lange (now of blessed memory) kept track of all those hundreds of books that publishers sent to *Religious Studies Review*, which I then assigned to our area editors to be assigned in turn to subeditors who assigned them to reviewers in various parts of the continent. Helen then mailed the books to those reviewers and duly recorded the reviews as they came in and ultimately sent copies of the reviews to the publishers. (Her motto: "When in doubt, send it out.") There were still other staff over the years to whom I remain very grateful—their names would fill another paragraph.

For me, *Religious Studies Review* meant—in between classes and other duties around the office and working on my dissertation plus responsibilities at home—close editing of every long review and every review note submitted to the journal and, with the long-time editorial chair, Mary Gerhart at Hobart and William Smith Colleges in Geneva, N.Y., proofreading galleys and then the page proofs. Since electronic transfers still lay in the future, she read me her corrections over the phone. It was all an ongoing education in itself, keeping me abreast (willy-nilly) of the whole field of religious studies from methodology and theory to sociology and psychology and philosophy of religion to the broad spectrum of religions, ancient and modern, in different parts of the world, and the various ways in which religion was being studied in the academy. Those ways were evolving as "religion" at the post-secondary level had come to mean study *about* religion rather than inculcation of religion; *Religious Studies Review* contributed to the developing conceptualization and taxonomy of the field. My editorial functions included organizing the annual meetings of the journal's editorial advisory committee in connection with the annual meetings mentioned above, where I presented the plans for the journal for the next year. (Meanwhile thinking, Who was I to sit down at table with such a who's-who in religious studies?) Mary Gerhart and I have set down some of this history in separate articles in the twenty-fifth-anniversary issue of *Religious Studies Review* (October 1990).

Meanwhile, Norman was tapped to be president of the University of Calgary. It seems he was destined by fate and character for such a position and, after retirement, to serve as chairman, president, and CEO of Alberta Natural Gas. President Neale Tayler appointed me to take Norman's place as director of WLU Press, and the CSR appointed me to succeed him as executive officer of the CSR, a position at times very political and stressful.[1]

Meanwhile, I had finished my dissertation (published soon thereafter) and received tenure. My daughter, Elise, was in teachers' college, my son, Justin, in high school. Empty nest was in the offing. The evening I was to set out for the 1981 annual meeting of the CSR in Chicago Carolyn died of metastasized breast cancer at the age of forty-eight. The months before her death had meant daily visits to the hospital, including one at Victoria Hospital in London, where I served as her secretary recording the grades and comments for the students in the practicum in early childhood education that she had been teaching while working at

---

1 The CSR was renamed the Council of Societies for the Study of Religion (CSSR). See further Remus, "For Such a Time as This: The Council of Societies for the Study of Religion 1969–2009," in Scott S. Elliott, ed., *Fieldwork: The Best of the CSSR Bulletin* (Equinox, forthcoming).

the Early Childhood Centre at the University of Waterloo. There was a memorial service in Keffer Chapel at Waterloo Lutheran Seminary, followed by a reception in Centre Hall. I thanked John Weir for coming. His reply was characteristic: "What are friends for?"

John knew that in the CSR and at the Press we had a policy of inclusive language. After one of those panty raids that Fred Nichols and Arthur Stephen mention in their contributions to this volume, John asked me to write a guide to inclusive language for the campus. It appeared as a small booklet in 1990 under the title *Equity in Communication: Guidelines.*

Meanwhile, I had become very active in the Canadian Society of Biblical Studies and in 1993 was elected president of the society. My presidential address drew on my research and publications that employed sociology of knowledge to examine the long history of debates about accounts of extraordinary phenomena in the ancient Mediterranean world, which one eminent scholar of my acquaintance summed up in his aphorism, "Your 'magic' is my 'miracle,' and vice versa." Putting on my hat as a student of the academic study of religion, I got involved in a series of books on the state-of-the-art of religious studies in Canada, taking me back to my graduate-school days of interviewing professors and students and analyzing data; two Queen's professors and I published the volume on Ontario.

I am ever grateful to those three amigos who carved out a job for me at WLU. Five years after Carolyn's death, Alice Croft and I were married. I married a Canadian, became a Canadian citizen, and am very fond of the country of my adoption—but will never be a fan of hockey until it trades in violence for skill.

Chapter 33

French House: A First, and Then Some

JOAN KILGOUR

𝒾 T IS JANUARY 1964. I AM INTO MY SECOND TERM OF COURSEWORK toward a master's degree in French at McMaster University. Though I have yet to finish the term and to write my thesis, the need to be looking for work in the fall strikes even a twenty-three-year-old. My professors mention casually to me that Waterloo Lutheran University is advertising a position as head resident in their new French House combined with a full-time lectureship in French. My innocent answer is, "Where is Waterloo Lutheran University?" And thus begins the tale.

It is very important to hang on to one's old scrapbooks. I applied for the position and still have the letter from Dr. Neale Tayler, chair of Romance Languages, inviting me for an interview in February (with instructions to call SH 4-8141 from the bus terminal). I was interviewed by Dr. Tayler and Dean Lloyd Schaus, and two weeks later was offered the position, effective September 1964. The salary was $5,500 per annum, with free living accommodation. I accepted. I brought to the position an M.A., a year's worth of teaching English in France, and a deep enchantment with the language, literature, and culture of France. My love of teaching and my appreciation of French language and culture have never left me.

"La Maison Française" was the brainchild of Neale Tayler and, indeed, the first of its kind on a Canadian university campus. Located in a converted house on Bricker Street (at the corner of the present-day Chancellor's Drive), the residence housed nine women honours French students committed to speaking only French in a small privileged group. They were even willing to pay a one-cent fine for language infractions. The students and I decorated the common areas (living room and kitchen) with café curtains, posters, and odd bits of furniture considered vaguely French. In the basement we installed a "bohemian nightclub" with low tables, cushions, red-checkered cloths and curtains, and the inevitable candles in wine bottles. But no wine, ever—this was Ontario 1964. The head resident's apartment consisted of furnished living room, bedroom, and bath. As I was only a few years older than the students, and none of them was in my classes, we developed an immediate rapport, with most of them opting to return for the years following.

French House was officially opened on November 14, 1964, by Harry Greb, chairman of the Board of Governors, in the presence of President Villaume, Dean Schaus, Dr. Tayler, the beaming residents, and myself. The opening included an invitation to an open house to tour the premises. I stayed for three years as head resident. Several years later, French House, along with the homes of some illustrious neighbours (Fred Nichols and Aarne Siirala), succumbed to demolition to make way for the rapid expansion of the seventies.

The other aspect of my appointment was as lecturer in French, involving twelve hours a week of teaching at various levels. Those were the days of fourteen-week semesters, and no one complained that four courses each term constituted an excessive burden. My assignment for September 1964 consisted of two sections of French 20 (grammar), French 30 (survey of the novel), and French 40 (survey of drama). This struck me as a great deal of preparation, especially as I would be spending the summer writing my thesis. Dr. Tayler readily acceded to my polite request for relief from French 30, giving me in its place three language tutorial hours. This action was typical of the generosity and academic freedom I experienced throughout my entire career: consultation in the assignment of courses and freedom of choice regarding teaching methods.

As it is not my purpose to write a history of the department, I will speak of my career in very general terms. Many of the readers of this book will recall my first colleagues: Neale Tayler as chair; Lorna Berman, Larry Dawson, Terry Scully, and Ilse Stewart. They were friendly, very helpful, and always accepted me as an equal, even when I decided not to pursue the Ph.D., for which I had done research in Paris for several summers on the plays of a minor eighteenth-century French dramatist. That I chose to remain at WLU, and was granted tenure, is in large part due to their encouragement.

With the expansion of the university in the seventies came internal changes. Romance Languages was split into French and Spanish, which later combined with German. I had the stimulating experience, sometimes challenging but always collegial, of working with new colleagues and chairs, and the sad experience of losing others. In my latter years, the various language groups were united as the Department of Languages and Literatures. These several configurations, along with the many necessary program innovations, assured our adaptability and cooperation.

Physical relocation was also a fact of life: from my living room office in French House I moved with my colleagues to Willison Hall, which also housed the library, and then to the Central Teaching Building (now Alvin Woods). The next relocation of the department was to McDonald House, a student residence temporarily transformed into faculty offices during the construction of the Aird Building. The impact of these relocations on my personal life was wonderful and enduring. The department subsequently spent several years in the Aird Building, then relocated to the Bricker Academic Building, where it remains—for the time being.

In 1964 WLU truly was a "small undergraduate university" with a federated seminary. My scrapbook yields an article proudly announcing that in May 1964 convocation was "the biggest ever, over 200 students." Another clipping reports a student population of 1,300; so there were probably some 100 faculty members. As one might expect, we all knew each other, as well as those in the administration, library, registrar's office, bookstore, and the custodial and dining-hall staff. I distinctly remember the annual spring marks meeting in room 1E1, when all faculty members met to discuss cases of students shy a mark or two of graduating or continuing on: "Could you raise this mark in Economics 230?" "French 40?" "Biology 250?"

I recall faculty retreats in early September designed to instruct and inspire; a particular two-day event at Jordan Harbour stands out in memory. In following years the administration offered one-day sessions of meetings and workshops, culminating in a banquet. Faculty members were also connected through lively WLU Faculty Association parties and the annual Waterloo County Cultural Tour, a.k.a. pub crawl. Finally, the faculty lounge located off the Torque Room was a common venue for small meetings and of course lunch and conversation. It is unfortunate that as the university grew bigger the lounge could no longer accommodate the increased number of faculty and that collegiality suffered from the inevitable fragmentation into divisional faculties.

I conclude with words I spoke at the "Celebrating Our Commitment" dinner of June 2000 to honour faculty and staff of twenty-five, thirty, and thirty-five years' service. "In 1964 I was suddenly involved in a teaching profession which, thirty-five years later, I love no less. To my family, friends, and colleagues: Thank you for the wonderful adventure." The adventure continues, and I'm still loving it.

Chapter 34

PERIPATETIC PEREGRINATIONS

ANDREW LYONS

66 ᴛ HAT'S THE STRANGE LITTLE PLACE THAT KEN HEWITT WENT
to," remarked Carmel Schrire, a Rutgers archaeologist, when I
told her that I'd be leaving New Jersey for Canada. "So you think they're
going to pay you real dollars," exclaimed another colleague, Robin Fox,
at a party in my honour. "They're going to pay you LIRE—Canadian
LIRE!" So how did I come to teach at the "strange little place," and, now
that I have retired, what can I say about my thirty-two years teaching
here and the career in anthropology that led me to Waterloo?

I entered anthropology because it seemed to be the furthest route
away from respectability. I had studied Classics in Leeds Grammar School
in the North of England. My parents warned me that my interest in
ancient history was not practical and that I would never get a job teaching it. Accordingly, I took a B.A. in law at Oxford in order that I might
follow one of the two family professions. (I was too uncoordinated for
medicine—there were fears that I would remove the wrong organs from
patients when my fingers slipped.) I spent four years instead of the usual
three on the degree. There were no electives and I was refused the opportunity to switch to political science. Bored stiff, I did little work, listened
to too many records, made many friends, and got involved in student
politics. In my last year as an undergraduate I decided to try postgraduate work in social anthropology.

I had a very outdated idea of what anthropologists did, but I had
observed that some of my lazier and more eccentric friends enjoyed

181

doing it. Miraculously, I passed my final exams in law with marks that did not bar me from postgraduate work. Rodney Needham, who later became the professor of Social Anthropology at Oxford but at that time was still the diploma secretary (i.e., admissions officer), took a gamble by allowing me to study for the one-year diploma in Social Anthropology. For the first two months that gamble seemed likely to come unstuck. It was then that I attended a party at the Anthropology Institute without my girlfriend, the daughter of a Tory MP, who had just dropped me in favour of a student with better social connections. At the party I met a wonderful person, a young American named Harriet David, who was one of the institute's best students. Within a month I was engaged to her and hard at work at my studies.

In July 1967 I secured a three-year scholarship and commenced a doctoral thesis on anthropology's role in the rise and fall of scientific racism, a topic that united my political and academic interests. I took far too much time, and was quite surprised when my wife suggested that I needed to get a job so that I would have something to do when my grant expired and an incentive to finish the thesis. Early in 1970 I applied for a position under a special scheme, the British Teacher Program, operated by the Woodrow Wilson National Fellowship Foundation and the English-Speaking Union. Successful applicants were placed with universities that had expressed an interest in hosting such young scholars and paying their salaries, which were free of income tax. I was one of the successful applicants because my supervisor, a very kind man, wrote positively about the imminent completion of the thesis that I had barely started, and because one of my friends was on the British interviewing panel. I got the position at Kent State University before I had met a single faculty member there. The dean of Arts and Sciences at Kent had applied to the program, suggesting a high salary for me because he was under the mistaken impression that the English-Speaking Union and the Woodrow Wilson Foundation would be paying it. Harriet was offered part-time teaching at Kent.

In February 1970 nobody had heard of Kent State University. "Why are you buying four newspapers?" asked the newsagent on Cowley Road in Oxford, when we sought mementoes of the shootings of four students at Kent State by the Ohio National Guard on May 4 of that year.

"Because we're going to teach there next year."

"Oh! Pity they can't do that here," said the newsagent, bemoaning a dearth of opportunities for slaughter.

"One, two, three, four, why not a hundred more?" That was a spray-painted sign on a wall on Main Street that greeted us on the hot September day we first set foot in Kent. During our first year as university teachers the Kent campus was visited by Phil Ochs, Jane Fonda, Joan Baez, Allen Ginsberg, and William Kunstler. Classes were regularly interrupted by bomb threats, particularly around mid-terms. Harriet and I worked hard at our teaching, and it proved to be an interesting and unexpected challenge. Kent had an open admissions system, and that policy resulted in the presence in the same large class of individuals who could not spell the third-person plural pronoun in English and a "faculty brat" (later a lifelong friend) who was to become an academic aide-de-camp to Chomsky in the MIT Linguistics department. In 1972 I took a year off to finish my thesis and Harriet took a full-time position at Kent. I had already received a teaching award (entirely a student initiative), so at the age of twenty-eight I had this honour, a chance of finishing the thesis, and no job. The thesis, however, was shapeless, and I worried because my supervisor had never read it in full. There was no committee system at Oxford, and my complaint was not unusual. Somehow the thesis was completed and I defended it in September 1974. The tome occupied two volumes and was more than five hundred pages long. The examiners passed it because they could not face having to read it again.

Meanwhile, I had been hired at Rutgers–Newark. This ghetto campus had some fine faculty and some very good students, but it was the poor cousin of the Rutgers system and it was certainly treated as such—there was not even money to bring in a commencement speaker. The politics were poisonous. The dean was accused of favouritism, and his sworn enemy, my department chair, secured his resignation (followed a year later by suicide) by a faculty motion establishing a review of college governance and by audible threats to reveal his sexual peccadilloes to all and sundry (so audible that this was what philosophers call a performative utterance). I joined a faculty seminar in social science at Columbia University in which the average age was about sixty-five. My work as their secretary provided some consolation for the miseries of the job. So too did my graduate teaching at the main Rutgers campus in New Brunswick, N.J., although this added to our commuting obligations.

Harriet had secured a job in Massachusetts, teaching in succession at the University of Massachusetts and then Smith College till 1980. We had a commuter marriage.

Until we developed a research project in Nigeria our library research was only modestly successful. Anthropology is a discipline in which empirical work (fieldwork) and theory are closely intertwined. Publishing purely in theory or in history of theory is not an established route, and there are fewer venues for publication. The change in our research direction was in part accidental. We had been asked to teach courses on Africa, and Oxford had given us training in Africanist anthropology. One day in the mid-seventies a friend whom we were visiting in New York showed us some Onitsha market pamphlets, a unique form of popular literature in English that was written by and for the first or second generation of young people to receive secondary education in eastern Nigeria. We resolved to do a project on the ways in which Nigerians fashioned modern selves through the media of books, magazines, newspapers, films, radio, and television. Such projects are now common, but they were not so in 1976, when we made our first trip to Benin City, once famous for its brass sculptures, divine kings, and imperial power. When Harriet and I returned to Benin to complete our study in 1983 and 1984, we were sharing a joint tenured position at Laurier, and Harriet was my department chair.

I had applied for jobs throughout North America in late 1976, because I needed to get out of Rutgers in order to do the research I wanted to complete and to secure tenure, which was uncertain there and not strongly desired. I responded to an advertisement for a position in anthropological theory posted at the American Anthropological Association meetings. I had never heard of Laurier, but the young department chair who interviewed me (Mat Guenther) was kind, modest, and brilliant. As part of the subsequent interview process, I gave a lecture—on a dreadful February day. Freezing rain covered the town, and one of the two taxicab companies refused to fetch me from the Waterloo Motor Inn. A portable was the grand venue for the lecture. I punctuated my talk with nervous puffs at my pipe (one could still smoke in buildings in those days), periodically suppressing the embers and putting my pipe in my pocket, from which smoke issued. As I wandered round the stage, I narrowly missed tripping on a step and several cables. The talk was entitled, "Why

Anthropologists Should Read *The Water Babies* by Charles Kingsley." I am not sure why I was hired.

Harriet was reluctant at first for me to take the job. However, once I had an offer she visited the campus and told me I had to take the position, even though it would mean a commute across an international boundary. Wilfrid Laurier at that time offered some things I really appreciated. The classes were small, and there was a chance to mentor good students on an individual basis. We taught the fourth-year students gratis, because there were rarely more than four of them to teach. About half of our honours students went to graduate school. My colleagues, Mat, Laird Christie (the "walking encyclopedia"), and Dean Knight were young and enthusiastic teachers. Over thirty years there were no quarrels between us. We were part of a joint Department of Sociology and Anthropology, which, despite occasional divisions, often united in resistance to the higher administration.

I had always wanted to teach at a "liberal arts college," and the Laurier of those days resembled many such small, church-related colleges in the United States. One got to know all the key players in the faculty and staff in very little time. Mat got me involved with the Laurier Festival committee, and I was able to meet many colleagues who became friends and to arrange visits by Ashley Montagu and Allen Ginsberg. There were disadvantages too, primarily male gender bias, extreme conservatism, and a lack of diversity. As Laurier has evolved into a multiversity, it has become a fairer place in many ways and it attracts some very good faculty, but it has lost that sense of intimacy shared by inhabitants of a small village. In 1980, Harriet joined us for a few years, ending our long years of commuting, when the university created the second shared appointment in Canada. She finished her teaching career just a few months ago as chair of Anthropology at the University of Waterloo.

After finishing our Nigeria project, we worked for many years on a project that was eventually to result in two books, *Irregular Connections* (2004) and *Sexualities in Anthropology* (2011). This was a return to historical research, which drew on my knowledge of the history of racism and inequality and Harriet's work on the anthropology of gender. Our work demonstrates the distortions in anthropological images of the sexuality of other peoples and shows how such refractions are often linked to disputes and contestations in our own society. Think of the South

Seas, of Bougainville, Gauguin, Somerset Maugham's *Rain,* and Margaret Mead! Meanwhile, Laurier bought Canada's oldest anthropology journal, *Anthropologica,* in 1989, and the efficient Wilfrid Laurier University Press began to publish it. Mat, Harriet, and another great colleague, Karen Szala-Meneok, joined me in editorial duties for eight years. It was then taken over by its rival, *Culture,* the Canadian Anthropology Society's journal, but a decision was made to retain the services of Laurier Press and the name *Anthropologica.* I am just finishing a three-year term as its editor-in-chief.

Laurier also gave me the opportunity to serve the departments of Sociology and Anthropology, the recently created Department of Anthropology, and the M.A. program in Cultural Analysis and Social Theory in various administrative capacities. I remain grateful for all these opportunities alongside the many other ways in which Laurier was my academic home for so many years.

Part Six

Arts and Culture

Chapter 35

Voices from the "Scales House": Music at WLU 1965–76

WALTER H. KEMP

*I*T WAS AN EARLY SPRING EVENING IN OXFORD, CHILLY AND DAMP, as would be expected. I had played for an international Lutheran conference in the Chapel of Mansfield College. Stepping out onto the Quad I noticed a slight gentleman wandering about rather forlornly. "I was looking for someplace to eat," he said (not an easy thing to find after 8 p.m. in those days).

"Are you from Germany?" I enquired, guessing at the accent that coloured his distinctively pleasant voice.

"No, I am from Canada."

"I am Canadian also; I'm a doctoral student here in musicology. Walter Kemp."

"Ah," he smiled. "My name is Ulrich Leupold, and I have been looking for you for over a year." And so was set in motion the sequence of arrangements and events that brought a twenty-six-year-old neophyte to Waterloo at the opening of the 1965–66 academic season as Waterloo Lutheran University's first full-time appointment in music.

I soon learned that the university was unprepared for the realities of actually doing music on campus. I was assigned an office on an upper floor in Willison Hall, assured that I would be welcome there so long as I did not make any noise. When they saw a middle-aged upright piano being trundled into my quarters, matters moved quickly. I was transferred, together with the piano, into a hastily constructed cubbyhole in the basement, next to the boiler room.

There were more appropriate facilities. The Theatre Auditorium offered a surprisingly functional stage with reasonably adequate resources for concerts and musical productions. Above the main lobby of the principal building was Room 3C15, a lecture theatre with a mini-platform, audio equipment, a small grand piano, and serviceable acoustics. This became the place where the choir rehearsed, where all the academic theory and history classes were taught, and where vocal and chamber music recitals eventually would nurture a taste for such repertoire on the part both of campus and community audiences. These, together with a larger lecture hall, were the settings that would enable music to blossom and flourish at WLU.

The headquarters of the fledgling Department of Music was a house on the corner of Albert and Bricker streets. The main floor front consisted of two offices—one for myself and one for the secretary. (Yes, we had been assigned a secretary!) Upstairs the bedrooms were converted into (non-soundproofed) studios. The department shared the facility with the marine division of the Biology department, Robert McCauley conducting his research on alewives in the basement. From time to time I carried gifts of freshly killed fish two blocks down Albert Street to our home on the corner of Central. This unique site of sea and song I dubbed the "Scales House." As soon as the dwelling next door became available, it was cleared to lodge a vocal studio and some practice rooms. The last steps in this progressive expansion of separate musical locations would be the conversion of the garage of what was once the president's house (at that time, Centre Hall) into the vocal studio and the installation of a new organ in Keffer Chapel at the seminary. Meanwhile, under the careful but devoted eye of University Librarian Erich Schultz, himself a keen music lover, a small vinyl and printed collection was taking shape in the new library.

What made these rudimentary facilities work for us was the dedicated enthusiasm of our full-time teaching staff—organist-composer Barrie Cabena, pianist Ralph Elsaesser, tenor and chamber choir director Victor Martens, subsequently baritone David Falk—and several talented part-time instructors. Their work was grounded on the positive attitude of the university's administration and faculty. Not only was there the desire but also the natural assumption that music as a performance and academic subject was an integral part of a small liberal arts university. Lutheran and Mennonite educational philosophies, work ethics, and aesthetic tastes guaranteed not only the acceptance of music on campus but also its dynamic growth from slender beginnings to a separate faculty.

Reflecting now, five decades after commencing those exciting Waterloo years, it seems to me that the drama of the evolution from "Lutheran" to "Laurier" had as a dominant theme a sequence of creative tensions: first, between competing strains within the Lutherans involved with the university (American governance and Canadian academia); then between conservative Canadian Lutheranism and the questioning of received religious values and worship expression evidenced in the 1960s and early 1970s; finally the accommodation between Lutheran and Mennonite approaches to the purpose and practice of university-level education. Steering music's way through these "close encounters" was an administrative education in itself. Dependent upon, and sympathetic to, my inter-denominational teaching colleagues in the university's constituent disciplines, I knew I would need their continuing support and acceptance of a performing art within a baccalaureate program. At the same time, I served a role in the American-based administration's push to cultivate the arts on campus for the improvement of the community's image of the university. The common regard for music mentioned earlier held in a positive balance the role of music in enhancing the university's public profile and enriching the academic program.

Both for the public relations of the university and the life experiences for the students involved, tremendous advantages were offered by the administration's policy of imitating the Lutheran colleges in the US, such as Augustana, St. Olaf, and Concordia, in sending their choirs on tour—in our case during February break week. We went through Lutheran country west of Waterloo and up into the Ottawa Valley; during the church's centennial year we visited Montreal and Quebec City; south of the border we sang on invitation at Gettysburg College and Duquesne and Pittsburgh universities, culminating at the magnificent Valparaiso University chapel, the unofficial cathedral of the Lutheran Church–Missouri Synod.

The heady years of the sixties were zestful for those of us involved in the university but unsettling for some of the university's Lutheran constituency: "God Is Dead," *The Gospel According to Peanuts*, the *Cotton Patch Version* New Testament, the experimental liturgies, the Beatles, Simon and Garfunkel, Bob Dylan. At WLU, Chaplain Richard Urdahl's colloquial versions of preaching texts, student theatre productions like *The Fantasticks* and *Gypsy*. Occasionally the activities of our choir produced some anxiety. Mambo Mass composer-pianist Eddie Bonnemere came up from New York, as did the minister to the jazz community there, John Gensel. As a continuing centennial-year project we commissioned Canadian composers to write choral works for us, William Brubacher of Waterloo Music Co. having the generosity and vision to publish these as the WLU Choral Series. Unfortunately, the works of John Beckwith, Norma Beecroft, and other composers disturbed some of our rural and small-town church audiences. One Lutheran pastor, after listening in on our rehearsal, held an impromptu hymn sing before our concert to mitigate what was to come. We were never invited back. In one small town outside of Waterloo I came upon the pastor lighting the altar candles to set the mood for our "concert of traditional sacred music," upon which I ran downstairs and whispered to the choir, "Kill the Quebec folk songs." Justice was visited upon us in any case with a tiny audience, explained to me by one of our students, baritone Dan Lichti, now an internationally renowned soloist and voice professor at WLU: "This was the night of their creamery party!" When the student barbershop quartet was included in a concert in a major Waterloo Lutheran church, the pastor complained to the university that if that is the way the students were going, the Lutheran church should have nothing to do with them. These were years of growing pains for religious worship and for the identity and function of an institution such as Waterloo Lutheran, but our students emerged stronger in spiritual and social values thanks to their engagement as singers in the university choir.

The 1970s brought a fresh tension of purpose, as the earnest tone of career-driven music students, many from other provinces, began to exert a counter-ethic to the amateurism-with-standards of the older Ontario Lutheran viewpoint upon which the department's growth had been based. The little church-affiliated university with a big heart would evolve into a not-so-little, equally warm-hearted provincial university, but one with a fresh vision of music, a deeply textured program focused on professional training, with the tools and the teachers to achieve the success that WLU's Faculty of Music would achieve.

Personalities who made Waterloo Lutheran University a memorable place come to mind. On my arrival I was welcomed by the then president,

Dr. William Villaume. He had an astute view of music's influence on the community's perception of the university. I am sure he appreciated music, his son being a solid trumpet soloist. I did wonder, however, why he would ask me how long a concert would take, and when it would finish. I found out. One night I was sitting upstairs in the Theatre Auditorium as he arrived to take his seat in full public view. As soon as the lights dimmed, I saw him quickly exit through the side door, only to return exactly five minutes before the final curtain, so as to be seen leading the applause. Our concert band conductor, Capt. Derek Stannard of the Royal Canadian Regiment Band of London, Ont., told me how Villaume praised his choice of march for the convocation ceremony. "Use it again, Derek; it embodies the spirit of Lutheranism!"

"We did for a while," said Derek, "even though it was *The March of the Charioteers* from the movie *Ben-Hur*."

I benefited a great deal from working with my administrative colleagues. Vice-President Dr. Henry Endress was a music devotee and a passionate supporter of choir tours and public concerts. From him I learned the value of marketing cultural affairs. Everything I learned about public relations—writing press releases, extracting key words for headlines, and placing the meat of a story in just the right place to be picked up by a headline writer—I acquired from WLU publicist Richard K. Taylor. Dick was a bundle of nervous energy, a more benign version of the gravedigger's characterization of Yorick as "a mad rogue." What he taught me about preparing copy for print media was backed up by insights in program layout and publishing by Taylor's co-worker George Thompson and his successor Barry Lyon—all valuable techniques employed in my later career in Halifax.

One critical item on page layout that I picked up from a negative example at that time was always to complete a sentence or paragraph at the conclusion of a page. It happened that the choir was singing at an academic awards night. The then chairman of the board, a lovely man and head of a nationally known local business, read his speech in a manner obviously indicating he had not created it. Coming to the bottom of the penultimate page he read, "In conclusion I would like to say ..." (only to find that the last page had been shuffled back into the pack). "In conclusion I would like to say ..." (desperate riffling of papers to find the missing finale). "In conclusion I would like to say ..." (page found) "how sincerely happy I am to be here."

The university comptroller, Tamara Giesbrecht, kept the institution afloat with a winning smile and an iron calculator. Fortunately, she too was sympathetic to campus music. I still call her *exempla* to mind when, as artistic director of Opera Nova Scotia, I am reconciling artistic ideals with economic realities. Carol Raymond, the department secretary, I had known as a community church musician; as I had confidently assessed, she turned out to be the model administrative coordinator. Certainly her experience in her former work as a loans officer was very effective in wresting late essays from students. Dr. Flora Roy, a most gracious lady and a great soul, exerted a profound influence on my academic teaching, revealing the possibilities of interdisciplinary studies in a manner that prepared me to participate confidently in the famous and exacting Foundation Year Programme at the University of King's College, Halifax.

I return full circle to Dr. Ulrich Leupold, a man of erudition and a musicologist, now featured prominently in Paul Helmer's recent book *Growing with Canada: The Émigré Tradition in Canadian Music* (2009), who devoted so much of his time to editing organ and choral pieces for parish use. He planned and implemented courses in basic theory, hymnology, organ technique, and playing in worship service, with an eye to improving the skill and knowledge of church musicians of all denominations. This holy man with a twinkle in his eye and a hymn in his heart is the finest model of Christian service I have been privileged to meet.

My last, and most lasting, memories are of the students, especially those amazing spirits who made up the university choir until 1976. When we met again at a reunion a few years ago, I found the repertoire so engrained in them that we pulled off a concert with one day's rehearsal. Some were church ministers; one was to become a senior Canadian Armed Forces chaplain; one had composed an opera; one was a university music librarian; many were teachers and homemakers. Individual members told me how much their undergraduate choir days had meant to them as they faced later crises of illness, marital breakup, and career difficulties: the fellowship and the singing had helped them through. These alumni represent the best of what Waterloo Lutheran University was about, and I always shall be grateful to have shared it with them. "Bliss was it in that dawn to be alive, / But to be young was very heaven!"

Chapter 36

The First Four Years: Foundations for the Next Thirty-Three

PAUL TIESSEN

*L*OOKING BACK ON MY 37 YEARS AT LAURIER, I REALIZE THAT MUCH took shape during my first four years—1974–78—just after Waterloo Lutheran had become Wilfrid Laurier. There was much talk about new directions and new visions—and much energy.

Growing up in Kitchener during the 1950s, I had always been aware of WLU. My dad taught non-credit evening classes at "Lutheran" and spoke of it as a feisty little place. When I began undergrad studies at the University of Waterloo in 1963, I heard about a mythic figure at Waterloo Lutheran, "Dr. Roy," the larger-than-life chair of English there.

In 2007, when I was honoured with the Alumni Association's Hoffmann-Little Award, I reflected on what Dr. Roy meant to me. I said that Flora Roy—then ninety-six years old and unable to attend the event—was present perhaps more than we knew, for she had affected the lives of all of us, if only indirectly. In my case, in 1965–66 she had aided in my conversion from math and psychology to English literature—and, by consequence, to the not-yet-invented area of film studies. My conversion occurred after transferring to Lutheran from its then affiliated Mennonite Brethren College of Arts in Winnipeg, where I had taken year two of my studies, and enrolled in a required English course taught by Jim Clarke. Made aware of my interest in the assigned readings, he immediately introduced me to Dr. Roy.

Suspecting that I might be at least a closet Mennonite, she told me that I would someday figure out how to live in the world and simultaneously be Mennonite. She suggested that English studies would benefit from someone trained in math. So I was off and running, first, into a makeup year (honours equivalent) in English at WLU, then in 1967 to graduate studies in English—and, unofficially, Film Studies—at the University of Alberta. There, my supervisor Sheila Watson reinforced Dr. Roy's push toward new scholarly frontiers and oversaw my research on the modernist literary community's complicated reception of "the movies." Meanwhile, most summers from 1969 to 1973 Dr. Roy gave me English courses to teach at "Lutheran."

During those early years, which coincided with Dr. Roy's last four years as chair, I ambitiously involved myself in starting up two literary projects that took off beyond expectations and in which I am still involved: the *Malcolm Lowry Review* and Sand Hills Books. "Yes," she said when I talked about founding a literary journal, "let's claim it as part of our department activity. But remember, you'll have to do the work yourself!"

In 1977 when the first issue of the journal appeared—at that time called the *Malcolm Lowry Newsletter*—she was immediately an avid supporter. And in 1977, when the first Sand Hills title appeared—*People Apart: Portrait of a Mennonite World in Waterloo County, Ontario*—she defended it in the face of criticism from higher up, where at first it had been mistaken for a religious tract.

Sand Hills published primarily little-known twentieth-century visual texts emerging from the work of Waterloo Region painters and photographers. It included books connected to the life and work of artist Woldemar Neufeld and led to the publication (or co-publication) of related titles beyond its own list, by university and other presses; for example, *Woldemar Neufeld's Canada: A Mennonite Artist in the Canadian Landscape 1925–1995*, published by WLU Press (2010), for which my wife Hildi Froese Tiessen of Conrad Grebel University College and I wrote the text.

The *Malcolm Lowry Review* grew over its twenty-five years to annual issues of over 200 pages. It served as a gathering place for up to 125 scholars from over twenty countries. It also spawned a subsidiary imprint: MLR Editions Canada, which published forgotten literary manuscripts, especially those linked to Lowry and his circle. It took on other large projects too, such as Gerry Noonan's 1997 biography, *Refining the Real Canada: Homer Watson's Spiritual Landscape*, and the 449-page experimental novel by Dallas Wiebe, *Our Asian Journey* (1997). Dr. Roy always applauded each volume, especially when she saw how much you could do for so little money and lots of sweat equity.

I have loved doing archival research over the years, and find that my work in what at first were little-known areas seems to have contributed to developing various kinds of scholarly discussion: Malcolm Lowry's writing in relation to Canadian and European modernism; minority-culture work by Mennonite writers and artists in relation to the Canadian mainstream; debates in the 1920s–70s in the UK and Canadian literary circles about "cinema."

That takes me back again to those early years, in 1973–74, when I was considering moving to Laurier from the University of Manitoba, where I was teaching English and Film Studies in my first tenure-track position. Dr. Roy had painted a picture of Laurier as an adventure in search of fresh vision and direction. She talked about the new Fine Arts program and the potential for a Communication Studies program. She talked about the art-historical and technical-production directions in which she was taking Film Studies. I loved the thought of getting in on the ground floor of new institutional energy and applied for the English and Film Studies job, feeling I would have a chance to give shape and momentum to the programs she was telling me about.

Dr. Roy had begun to establish Film Studies as a concentration of a couple of "English" courses during the late 1960s when she brought Willi Nassau to WLU. I was shocked to discover, upon my arrival at Laurier in 1974 from Manitoba (where support for Film Studies was widespread, enthusiastic, and grandly given), that not everyone at Laurier supported Film Studies, even in our own department. Luckily, right after Dr. Roy's retirement, I was able to draw strength from people in other departments—Jim Blackburn in Physics, Boyd McDonald in Music—who defended it as much as she had or as much as her successor, Gary Waller, had.

At first I felt it was not safe to work with popular "Hollywood" films and concentrated on international modernists. By 1978 I had taught work by directors such as Antonioni, Borowczyk, Buñuel, Cocteau, De Sica, Fellini, Godard, Kozintsev, Kurosawa, S. Ray, Renoir (whose *Rules of the Game* is one of my favourites), Resnais, Rossellini, Tati, Trnka, and Truffaut.

For the first twenty-five years we were refused space in the library for students to study films. And for some years during the 1990s I was not allowed to darken a classroom to screen films. In the 1980s Jan Uhde at the University of Waterloo and I put together a collaborative Film Studies program that we maintained for over two decades. In the early 2000s, with strong and brilliant leadership from my new colleague Philippa Gates and, by that time, firm and widespread support from our whole department (sporting its new name, English and Film Studies) and the university's senior administration, Film Studies developed a lively honours stream and, more recently, with the hiring of more excellent new colleagues, a Ph.D. program.

During my first years at Laurier, conversations involving various people about pushing the university toward more supple spaces for internal development (in university and department policies, in curricula, in pedagogy) and toward more supple links with the broader community (from the local to the international) were packed with projects, ideas, breakthroughs, and, occasionally, difficulty and distress, disappointment and opposition, turbulence and failure.

One place where a great deal of new thinking occurred was in committees, where I met terrific people from across the university. During that early 1974–78 period, I began years of service on many committees, including the Arts and Science Curriculum Committee, which helped to bring in many new courses and programs. There were also WLU Faculty Association committees with lively discussions and rethinking of Laurier's past, present, and future. One committee that I chaired almost did me in, however: the vice-president: academic's committee on calendar revision (1979–80). The work seemed endless, with people jockeying for pride of place in the calendar and some strong opposition to change. Still, in having to rethink the entire undergraduate calendar—design, layout, and structure—I learned just about everything there was to know about undergrad studies.

A little later, when I sat on Senate (1982–87) and chaired the Senate Committee on Research and Publications I was particularly pleased that—with a well-timed push from Gerry Noonan—we got the university to provide more financial support for the arts on campus, especially in music, fine arts, and theatre. In the 1990s my support of the fine arts led to my serving on such university committees as Edna Staebler

Literary Awards (1989–94), Sculpture Selection (1990–91), and Aesthetics (1990–94). When Aesthetics Committee members took one of their zigzagging hikes through campus, in pursuit of President Lorna Marsden's quest for a pastoral "walk" that could be marked on a map, I suggested that "meanderthal" might work as a name for it. Luckily, few people heard my suggestion.

Early on, I chaired the university Art Committee and the Senate Cultural Affairs Committee (for which I published a Laurier events brochure each term) and for quite a while was a member of the university Festival Committee, once a year working with colleagues throughout the university who worked tirelessly to bring exciting week-long events to campus. Those kinds of involvements led to my—and others'—running a series of film festivals during the 1970s and 1980s. During the 1980s, Leslie O'Dell from our department began tapping the university's capacity for large-scale theatrical events, including musicals like *Guys and Dolls*, in which I had a small role where I could do but little damage.

Some of my efforts in "arts and culture" might have seemed quixotic to the administration. Vice-President: Academic Neale Tayler and Dean Gerald Vallillee sent polite responses to my sketches for a possible new arts complex along University Avenue that would be a home for live theatre, public film screenings, music concerts, and an art gallery. Later I proposed that a staircase encased in glass be put outside the Woods building—I have no idea how far that went, but we did get such a staircase!

Membership on some of these interdepartmental committee interests became major commitments. My hands-on work on three very busy interdepartmental committees—Fine Arts (1983–99), Communication Studies (1987–2000; coordinator, 1987–1992), and Canadian Studies (1975–97)—add up to over half a century!

Within the department I coordinated Film Studies from 1980 to 2002, chaired English from 1988 to 1997, and was coordinator of our co-op program for 16 of the years between 1980, when it was launched, and 2002. Co-op programs began with a special push from John Weir, who was interested in making Laurier competitive with other universities (notably Waterloo, a worldwide leader in co-op studies) in the search for the best high school students.

Now that classes are over for the last time, I dearly miss not only my colleagues but also my students. The students in my winter 2011 fourth-year seminar ("Modernism, Film, and Mass Media") evidently sensed my anxiety about heading into post-Laurier life and performed with exceptional brilliance, generosity, and grace. They daily reminded me how much I love classroom teaching, indeed, how much I have come to love it increasingly during the past ten years. Students seem livelier and more self-confident and expressive than ever, and I feel blessed for having shared their pursuit of intellectual and personal adventure.

In April 2011 many former students gathered at a reunion hosted by Philippa Gates to mark the thirtieth anniversary of Film Studies as a major and to celebrate Laurier's 100th birthday. Willi Nassau, about to celebrate his ninetieth birthday, was also present. A week later, students, having conspired with Philippa and Hildi and others, surprised me with an extraordinary farewell party. Through my tears and laughter, I realized that they had figured out a way to get me to transform my sense of retirement as a dreaded abyss into a broad vista, filled with potential. They sent me home with an eighty-page "Book of Memories, Comments, and Quotations" that they had created under the guidance of Kevin Hatch and Wendy Nind. I am grateful for and will miss deeply the practical inspiration and example of my students—as also of my colleagues. The parties and celebrations included a warm and wonderful dinner gathering of our whole department at the Sole restaurant where, alongside my long-time colleague Michael Moore, who was also retiring, I said my reluctant farewells.

During the last term I was awarded the Faculty of Arts Teaching Scholar Award with the opportunity to direct $1,000 toward a university project. I suggested the George & Agnes Roy Award, established for students enrolled in the double honours program Communication Studies and Film Studies, which Dr. Roy was central in initiating and an award that she had established in memory of her parents.

Our department has always been an exciting place. Mostly, we are a happy and productive community, now more than twice as large as when I arrived. Without knowing it, perhaps, the department lives with the generous and eclectic wisdom modelled by Dr. Roy. Starting from my year one, Hildi, upon receiving an invitation from Dr. Roy, taught at Laurier with me, part-time for eleven years, then full-time for two. When she was invited by Conrad Grebel University College to become its academic dean and first director of Graduate Studies in 1987, Dr. Roy made sense of it all immediately, saying that Hildi had been well trained at Laurier to do the job.

Dr. Roy flourished during her retirement, retiring twice, in fact, the second time from many years of part-time teaching while I was serving as department chair. Retirement opened new vistas for her and led her to publish her witty two-volume memoir about her life at Laurier: *Recollections of Waterloo College* (2004) and *Recollections of Waterloo Lutheran University 1960–1973* (2006). I suspect that, just as she had when Hildi was off to her new position, Dr. Roy, seeing me take up new rounds of post-institutional research and writing and publication on Lowry and others (and threatening someday to take up, perhaps, a round or two of golf), would have made sense of it all by saying that I had been well trained at Laurier to do the job.

Chapter 37

Remembering Maureen Forrester

GORDON GREENE

T HE CIRCUMSTANCES THAT PROMPTED WLU TO INVITE MAUREEN
Forrester to assume the role of university chancellor in the 1980s
had much to do with Dr. John Weir's vision of the university. He was an
economist by training and the former chair of Economics in the School
of Business and Economics; but when he became vice-president: academic in the 1970s he was concerned that the increasing prominence of
the school within the university might diminish the visibility of other faculties and departments.

I arrived at Laurier in 1978, having served as a department chair in
the Faculty of Music at the University of Western Ontario. The first
dean of the Faculty of Music at Laurier, Christine Mather, issued the
invitation to me to come to WLU and teach music history. When she
chose to accept an appointment in Victoria, B.C., in 1979, Dr. Weir saw
me as a person with at least a sliver of administrative experience and
asked me to serve as acting dean for the year while a search was undertaken. After a few months of "acting," I decided to add my name to the
search and was appointed dean in 1980, the same year Dr. Weir became
president succeeding Dr. Neale Tayler. It was then that I started sens-
ing Dr. Weir's unease concerning the imbalance of programs that
appeared to be developing. He started hinting that music served as a
kind of counterbalance to business. After all, singing and music generally were an integral part of the Lutheran traditions at the root of
the institution.

At that time the Faculty of Music occupied the MacDonald Hall residence with a classroom portable out back. A new building was needed if the program were to flourish. Chancellor John Black Aird's extensive connections in the political and financial world helped raise the funds, the new building was completed, and his name was assigned to the edifice. As Mr. Aird's successor as chancellor Dr. Weir and the Board of Governors chose Maureen Forrester, who at the time was serving as chair of the Canada Council. This was another significant, though subtle, effort to create breadth and balance in Laurier's programs.

Ms. Forrester was no stranger to Laurier, having conducted vocal workshops for Victor Martens' and David Falk's exceptional singing students for several years. Though serious, disciplined work had been required for the career she had developed as a world-renowned mezzo, she had a free, spontaneous, often jocular attitude about her role as chancellor. At meetings of the Board of Governors Ms. Forrester was a delightfully exuberant spirit. While serving in the chancellor's role at convocations she often chatted with graduates as their turn came to appear before her. Dr. Weir must have found her puzzling, perhaps intimidating at times, since he asked me to drive her to convocation ceremonies that were then held in the Kitchener Auditorium. He excused himself saying, "Gordon, you would be a better conversation partner than I could manage to be."

Naming the new recital hall after Maureen Forrester was a matter of great pride for faculty members in music. We had all argued forcibly that facilities for music required special acoustical treatment, hence, "Let's not build until we know it will be done properly." There were troublesome issues such as the close proximity to University Avenue's traffic noise. Dr. Weir agreed with our insistence that when CBC recording technicians came to test the recital hall the noise meter must read zero. And that goal was accomplished. Ms. Forrester, while performing an inaugural recital, expressed her pleasure at having her name on the fine new hall.

Does her association with Laurier end there? Not at all. An unfortunate array of circumstances compounded to create a further very significant association. She became ill and about the year 2000 was unable to continue performing. Throughout her life she had been so supportive of and generous toward arts organizations of all kinds, as well as individual artists, that she was essentially broke. Since their mother needed constant care, her five children agreed that the best arrangement was a nursing home. In an effort to assist with the cost as well as preserve their mother's library and the awards and documents acquired during her stellar career, they searched for a purchaser. After one or two abortive attempts, Professor Leslie De'Ath and Dean Charles Morrison of the Faculty of Music made an offer to at least receive all the material from storage in Toronto and display it in an orderly fashion.

It is an unusual collection. Not only is there a sizeable library of musical scores with her performance markings, including more than twenty compositions written for and dedicated to her, there are also boxes of year-by-year concert programs and reviews from 1950 on. There are also numerous photographs of her in various operatic roles and with groups of influential friends. Sixteen framed honorary doctoral diplomas grace the collection as well.

A fundraising effort was undertaken to acquire the entire collection for Laurier. When I was asked to resume the role of dean while Dr. Morrison was on leave in 2005–06, President Bob Rosehart made a decision: Laurier would buy the library now because the family needed the support, but fundraising would continue. I had the pleasure of delivering the cheque to the family in Toronto.

Earlier that year I realized it was Ms. Forrester's birthday in July, her seventy-fifth. I called her daughter, Gina Dineen, with whom negotiations about the collection were proceeding, suggesting that I would like to bring birthday greetings from WLU to her mother, since I had such fond memories of her as our chancellor.

"Gordon, she wouldn't know you," Gina said. "She doesn't recognize her own grandchildren."

Ms. Forrester's late husband, Eugene Kash, a distinguished Montreal violinist, was Jewish. When she passed away in June 2010 her family held a shiva celebrating her life at the home of her daughter Paula Berton in Toronto, to which I was invited. It was with deep feelings of respect and admiration that I expressed WLU's sympathy and my own to her family. And how proud and grateful we were that the memory of this Grand Dame of Song, exuberant chancellor, and great Canadian was being sustained in perpetuity at Wilfrid Laurier University.

About the Editors and Contributors
~

The Editors

ROSE BLACKMORE was a member of the faculty of the Graduate School of Social Work (later renamed the Faculty of Social Work) from 1970 to 1993. She has been a member of the WLU Retirees Association almost since its inception and served for many years on the executive committee.

BOYD MCDONALD taught piano, harmony, and counterpoint in the Faculty of Music 1976–1996. He became interested in the fortepiano in 1980 and has since recorded Beethoven, Brahms, and Molique using various fortepianos. Following retirement, he taught piano part-time until 2008 and served for many years on the executive of the WLU Retirees Association.

HAROLD REMUS came to WLU in 1974, teaching in Religion and Culture and as adjunct faculty in Waterloo Lutheran Seminary; he served as director of Wilfrid Laurier University Press (1978–83) and as executive officer of the Council on the Study of Religion (1977–85) when its office was located at WLU. He retired as professor emeritus in 1994.

The Editorial Committee

ROBERT ALEXANDER taught philosophy at WLU from 1964 to 1984, including four years as chair of the department. Since retiring from the Ontario civil service in 2002, he has been teaching courses for the Laurier Association for Lifelong Learning.

LOREN CALDER was born in Trail, B.C., in 1929. He joined the WLU Department of History in 1960, where he taught Russian, Soviet, and modern·diplomatic history, serving at times as department chair; he retired in 1994.

JOAN (WEBER) KILGOUR taught French language, literature, and culture at WLU from 1964 until her retirement in 2007.

FRANK MILLERD joined the Department of Economics in 1970, serving as chair of the department from 1987 to 1993 and as university secretary from 1994 to 1999. He retired in 2006.

BALDEV RAJ, professor emeritus, School of Business and Economics, came to WLU in 1972. The former editor of *Empirical Economics*, he was honoured as university research professor for 1989–90 and has held visiting professorships in the UK, Norway, Austria, Australia, Japan, New Delhi, and Canada, and now serves on the executive of the WLU Retirees Association.

The Photographer

JAMES HERTEL began his career at WLU on September 1, 1977, after being hired by Dr. Flora Roy and Willi Nassau with the title of University Photographer, retiring in 2009 from a career he had always dreamed of.

The Authors

JOHN ARNDT graduated from WLU in 1964; the holder of the B.L.S and M.L.S. degrees from the University of Toronto, he came to the WLU library in 1967, where he served variously as head of information services, collections management, and acquisitions. He retired in 1999.

DOREEN ARMBRUSTER began at WLU in 1973 in Academic Publications, the forerunner of Wilfrid Laurier University Press (established 1974). Production Coordinator for two decades until retiring in 1998, she continues as a freelancer on the production of the Press's sixteen-volume *Collected Works of Florence Nightingale*.

ED BENNET taught in the WLU Department of Psychology from August 1971 until his retirement in June 2005. He introduced community psychology courses and community-service learning at WLU and served as the director of the Community Psychology M.A. program for many years.

HART BEZNER obtained B.Sc. and Ph.D. degrees in physics from McMaster University. He was a member of WLU's Department of Physics from 1967 until retiring in 2003, during which time he also served for twenty-three years as director of Computing Services.

RALPH BLACKMORE (1916–2002) began teaching economics in the School of Business and Economics in 1966 after serving as financial editor at *The Globe and Mail* and in public relations at Massey Ferguson. He retired from WLU in 1981 and again in 1991. The Ralph Blackmore Award is given annually to a first-year student in honours Economics.

TERRY COPP joined the Laurier Department of History in 1975, retiring in 2004 to become director of the Laurier Centre for Military Strategic and Disarmament Studies, a position he still holds.

PETER C. ERB was a student in Honours English at WLU from 1961 to 1965, taught in the English 10 program in 1966–67, in the Department of English 1971–1984, and in the Department of Religion and Culture 1984–2008. In 1989 he was honoured with Laurier's Outstanding Teacher Award.

PAUL FISCHER, after nine years in parish ministry, served as manager of the WLU bookstore from 1965 until 1994.

BRUCE FOURNIER joined the School of Business and Economics in 1978, after seventeen years spent hunting submarines and conducting personnel research in the military. In addition to teaching management and organizational behaviour he served as associate dean and in the Research Centre for Management of New Technology and in the Laurier Institute for the Study of Public Opinion and Policy. He retired in 2002.

TAMARA GIESBRECHT began in accounting at WLU in 1960, became comptroller in 1963, and vice-president: finance in 1967, retiring in 1978. She was also a member of the Board of Directors of Equitable Life Insurance Co. from 1970 to 2002.

DELTON GLEBE (1919–2011) graduated from Waterloo College (1947) and Waterloo Lutheran Seminary (1950). He chaired the Board of Governors when Waterloo Lutheran University was established, taught at the seminary and university 1960–2002, and served as the principal-dean of the seminary 1970–84.

BARRY GOUGH joined the Department of History in 1972. He was university research professor and served as assistant dean of Arts and Science. In 2004 he retired to Victoria, B.C., as professor emeritus.

GORDON GREENE joined WLU as professor of music history in 1978. A year later he became dean, serving for ten years, and again in 2005–06. The Aird Building was constructed during his tenure in the 1980s.

REGINALD A. HANEY taught law in the School of Business and Economics from 1970 to 1995 and also served as university solicitor for a period of fifty years, from 1960 to 2010.

ALFRED HECHT taught in the Department of Geography and Environmental Studies from 1972 to 2006 and served as director of Laurier International from 1999 to 2005.

RAY HELLER was a faculty member in the Department of Chemistry from 1966 until his retirement in 1997, teaching various levels of introductory, organic, and industrial chemistry as well as biochemistry.

WALTER H. KEMP began at Waterloo College in 1965, coordinating and developing musical activities. These led to the founding of the Department of Music, of which he was chair until it became the Faculty of Music in 1975. During those years he presided over the implementation of the Bachelor of Music program and the expansion of the faculty roster. He also directed the WLU choir.

ANDREW LYONS taught in the Department of Sociology and Anthropology from 1977 to 2004 and in the Department of Anthropology from 2004 to 2009.

BILL MARR was a faculty member in the Department of Economics from 1970 to 2009 and served as assistant dean of Graduate Studies and

Research, associate director of Instructional Development, and chair of the Research Ethics Board during parts of those years.

ROBERT W. McCAULEY was a member of the original Biology department of Waterloo Lutheran University, joining in 1965 and continuing on into the Laurier years until retiring in 1992. He taught aquatic ecology and carried out research on the role of temperature in the life of fish.

JOSEPHINE C. NAIDOO joined the Department of Psychology in 1969, retiring at the rank of professor in 1997. Alongside professorial duties she was involved in a wide range of activities at WLU as well as at local, national, and international levels; in retirement she served as president of the WLU Retirees Association.

WILHELM E. (WILLI) NASSAU began at WLU in 1969 as director of Audio-Visual Resources; in addition he taught courses in film and other media. One of the founders of Telecollege, he retired in 1989.

RICH NEWBROUGH started at WLU in 1968 as an assistant football coach and lecturer in Physical Education. He became head football coach and director of Athletics in 1984, retiring in 1997. He coached the WLU football team that won the 1991 Vanier Cup.

FRED NICHOLS served as dean of students from the time of his arrival on campus in 1963 until 1997. The Campus Centre now bears his name; in retirement he assists the WLU development office in fundraising.

ARTHUR (ART) READ taught in the WLU Department of Physics and Computer Science from 1966 to 2005. After serving as dean of Arts and Science from 1983 until 1998, he was named as the first dean of the new Laurier Brantford satellite campus, serving from 1998 to 2000.

ROBERT J. (BOB) REICHARD found a home at Laurier for twenty years (1976 to 1996), as manager of Materiel Management, which included many hat changes along the way.

EDUARD RICHARD RIEGERT was professor of homiletics at Waterloo Lutheran Seminary 1965–1996 and Affiliated Faculty in Religion and Culture, WLU, 1970–1988.

ARTHUR STEPHEN joined Laurier in 1974 as a junior admissions officer. Over the next twenty years he was director of liaison, director of institutional relations, and in his last fifteen years as vice-president: advancement was responsible for recruitment, public affairs, alumni, and development. He retired in January 2011.

PAUL TIESSEN taught in the Department of English (now the Department of English and Film Studies) from 1974 until his retirement in 2011, serving as chair for three terms (1988–97).

FRANK TURNER was appointed in 1966 as the first full-time faculty member after the dean in the Graduate School of Social Work. He served as dean (1969–79) as well as acting vice-president: academic for one year. Following stays at Laurentian, York, and Case Western, he returned to Laurier to serve as interim dean of Social Work (1994–96), following which he served as head of Laurier International for one year.

HERBERT WHITNEY joined the WLU Department of Geography, Geology and Planning in 1965, where he taught historical/cultural geography, East Asia, environmental perception, and history and philosophy of geography. He retired in 1993.

JIM WILGAR received his B.A. from Waterloo Lutheran University (1960) and an M.A. in geography and resource management (1972). He served as director of admissions and liaison at WLU until 1970, when he became director of admissions at the University of Western Ontario; in 1977 he returned to WLU as registrar and secretary of senate. From 1984 until his retirement in 1997 he served as associate vice-president: student services and personnel.

I Remember Laurier: Photo Album

President William Villaume

Presidents Neale Tayler, John Weir, Frank Peters

Chancellor Maureen Forrester

Tamara Giesbrecht (Finance), Chancellor John Aird

More photos can be found at www.wlu.ca/retirees.

John Arndt (Library)

Robert Langen (Philosophy and Fine Arts)

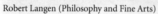

Walter Kemp (Music)

Arlene Greenwood (Computing)

Eric Schultz (Librarian)

Paul Fischer (Bookstore)

Arthur Stephen (Advancement)

Doreen Armbruster (Wilfrid Laurier University Press)

James Wilgar (Registrar's Office)

Murray Corman (Printing and Mail Services), seated; standing, l. to r.: Betty Goldie, Hertha Krueger, Don Doyle, Dale Weber, Dorothy Weppler, Barbara Linder

Willi Nassau (Audiovisual)

Bob Reichard (Materiel Management)

Fred Nichols (Dean of Students)

James Hertel (University Photographer)

Gerry Donelle (Shipping and Receiving)

Herbert Whitney (Geography)   Russell Muncaster (Geography)

Delton Glebe (Seminary)   Boyd McDonald (Music)

Eduard Riegert (Seminary)

Victor Martens (Music)

Edcil Wickham (Social Work)

Frank Turner (Social Work)

Rose Blackmore (Social Work)

Gordon Greene (Music)

Reginald Haney (Business)

Max Stewart (School of Business and Economics)

Herman Overgaard (School of Business and Economics)

Rich Newbrough (Physical Education)

Mathias Guenther (Anthropology)

Baldev Raj (Economics)

Bill Marr (Economics)

Welf Heick (History)

Peter Erb (English)

Frank Millerd (Economics)

Barry Gough (History)

John McMenemy (Political Science)

Harold Remus (Religion and Culture; Wilfrid Laurier
University Press)

Terry Copp (History)

Alfred Hecht (Geography)

Hart Bezner (Physics and Computing)

Flora Roy (English)

Joyce Lorimer (History)

Paul Tiessen (English)

Josephine Naidoo (Psychology)

Donald Morgensen (Psychology)

Ray Heller (Chemistry)

Ed Bennett (Psychology)

Russell Rodrigo (Chemistry)

Norman Wagner (Graduate Studies;
Wilfrid Laurier University Press)

Arthur Read (Physics), Joseph Guido (technician)

Robert McCauley (Biology)

Frederick Binding (Psychology)

Loren Calder (History)

Robert Alexander (Philosophy)

Back row, l. to r., Joan Kilgour (French), with residents of French House; Harry Greb (Chair, WLU Board of Governors); President William Villaume. Front row, Neale Tayler (Chair, Romance Languages)